THE
COOKIE
COOKBOOK

To Staci
From Uncle Steve
Christmas
1997

THE
COOKIE
COOKBOOK
LORNA RHODES

PHOTOGRAPHS BY SUE JORGENSEN

LONGMEADOW
PRESS

Published by Longmeadow Press
201 High Ridge Road, Stamford CT 06904

Cover and interior design by
Peter Bridgewater

ISBN: 0-681-45460-1

PRINTED IN ITALY
FIRST LONGMEADOW PRESS EDITION

0 9 8 7 6 5 4 3 2 1

CONTENTS

◆ ◆ ◆

INTRODUCTION

❖ ❖ ❖

Everyone loves freshly baked cookies – the delectable aroma of baking is so irresistible. As well as being pleasurable to eat, cookies are easy and fun to make and, with so many different ingredients to combine together, the variety of cookies is almost endless.

This book is a collection of some of the many cookies that can be created at home for a fraction of the cost of bought ones; it is surprising just how many can be made from a small amount of mixture. Make them for family and friends, or give as a present; wrapped in pretty paper, they make popular gifts, especially during the holidays.

Cookies are also ideal to make for fund-raising events. The ingredients need not be expensive, but the rewards are great and home-made cookies always sell out fast, which proves their appeal.

HINTS ON INGREDIENTS

The recipes in this book use everyday ingredients that can be bought in most supermarkets. Always choose good-quality fresh ingredients when buying butter, nuts and chocolate. Measure ingredients carefully, because the amounts given in the recipes are balanced to give good results. Be guided by the yield stated in the recipe; if you make many less or more, they may turn out too large or too small.

BUTTER: Many recipes call for sweet unsalted butter, which has a fresh and creamy taste and gives an excellent flavor and result. Some recipes that would normally have salt added use salted butter instead, and a few others use margarine. Butter always gives a better flavor but margarine can be used if a vegetable fat is preferred. For best results have butter and eggs at room temperature (unless otherwise stated).

SUGARS: The recipes always indicate the type of sugar to use. Many use unrefined brown sugars, which have more flavor and give tastier results than refined brown sugar. Raw sugar needs to be sifted, as often small lumps form during storage. Golden superfine and granulated sugar have a subtle buttery flavor, which will make cookies particularly delicious. If unrefined sugar is not available, then white sugar or soft light and dark brown sugar can be used.

CHOCOLATE: When choosing chocolate for these recipes, always use a good-quality one with a high cocoa solids content. Avoid cake-covering types of chocolate; these have a high sugar and vegetable fat content and will not give good results. Handle carefully when melting; warm slowly so as not to overheat.

PREPARATION HINTS

When making creamed mixtures you can use a wooden spoon, electric mixer or food processor. It is important not to over beat, because if the mixture is overworked, it will become too soft, and the cookies will spread too much during baking. Add dry ingredients carefully, using the pulse on food processors to avoid overworking the dough.

Check your oven manufacturer's handbook for any instructions on shelf positions. Generally, for gas ovens, the top half will give best results, electric ovens need to be pre-heated before baking and fan-assisted ovens will bake four sheets of cookies at a time. Check temperatures, as fan-assisted ovens need to be turned down slightly and generally cook more quickly. Baking times in recipes are given as a guide; every oven differs slightly in temperature, so check cookies before the stated cooking time is up.

CLASSIC COOKIES

The easiest cookies to make in this chapter are "drop" cookies, for which the soft dough is spooned directly onto the baking sheet. Drop cookies tend to spread during baking and the shape will often be irregular. The texture is also variable; it can be soft and chewy or crisp, like the popular Double Chocolate Chip Cookies.

Shaped cookies, such as Ginger Snaps and Honey Jumbles are also very straightforward to make – the dough is molded with cool hands, but care must be taken not to overhandle the mixture as the dough will toughen during baking.

For rolled mixtures, such as Vanilla Sugar Cookies, the dough must be stiff and often requires chilling so that you can roll it evenly before using a cutter. Too much flour used in rolling out will result in tough cookies. When no liquid is added, for example in shortbread, the mixture will require plenty of kneading before it is rolled out. The thinner you roll the dough, the crisper the baked cookies will be.

Piped cookies look very special and require a little more time and skill. Metal tips give a more defined shape than plastic. Alternatively the dough can be pressed out with a mechanical cookie press.

Refrigerator dough is a useful standby to have so that cookies can be baked at your convenience. A wide variety of flavorings can be used in the dough, which is chilled until it is firm enough to be cut into thin slices.

CONTENTS

◆ ◆ ◆

DOUBLE CHOCOLATE CHIP COOKIES

These classic cookies, with their soft chewy texture, are absolutely delicious eaten warm. They crisp up when cooled and have a rich chocolaty flavor.

◆ ◆ ◆

$1/3$ CUP BUTTER OR MARGARINE

$1/3$ CUP GOLDEN SUPERFINE SUGAR

$1/2$ CUP SIFTED RAW SUGAR

1 LARGE EGG, BEATEN

1 TEASPOON VANILLA EXTRACT

$1\,1/4$ CUPS SELF-RISING FLOUR

3 TABLESPOONS UNSWEETENED COCOA

$1/4$ CUP FINELY CHOPPED WALNUTS

$3/4$ CUP DARK CHOCOLATE CHIPS

MAKES ABOUT 16

◆ ◆ ◆

Put the butter or margarine into a bowl with the sugars. Beat together until fluffy, add the egg and vanilla extract, and beat well again.

Sift together the flour and cocoa and fold into the mixture with the walnuts and three-quarters of the chocolate chips.

Drop heaped teaspoonfuls of the mixture onto greased baking sheets. Flatten slightly, then sprinkle over the rest of the chocolate chips.

Bake at 350°F for 15 minutes. Cool for 2 minutes, then transfer to a wire rack to cool completely.

BANANA PECAN COOKIES

Children will love the nutty banana taste of these cookies. The banana makes them slightly moist and chewy.

◆ ◆ ◆

$1/2$ CUP BUTTER OR MARGARINE

$3/4$ CUP GOLDEN GRANULATED SUGAR

1 LARGE EGG

2 TABLESPOONS DARK RUM OR ORANGE JUICE

1 MEDIUM RIPE BANANA, MASHED

2 CUPS ALL-PURPOSE FLOUR

$1/2$ TEASPOON BAKING POWDER

1 CUP CHOPPED PECAN NUTS

PECAN NUT HALVES TO DECORATE

MAKES ABOUT 26

◆ ◆ ◆

Beat together the butter or margarine with the sugar until creamy. Add the egg and rum or orange juice and beat again. Mix in the banana.

Sift the flour and baking powder together, mix in the nuts, then add to the creamed mixture.

Drop heaped rounded teaspoonfuls onto greased baking sheets and press a pecan half onto each. Bake at 325°F for 18-20 minutes until lightly browned. Cool for 2-3 minutes, then transfer to a wire rack.

TOP: *Banana Pecan Cookies*
BOTTOM: *Double Chocolate Chip Cookies*

LEMON SHELLS

These light cookies have a lovely tangy lemon flavor and make a perfect partner to either tea or coffee.

◆ ◆ ◆

$1/2$ CUP SOFT MARGARINE

5 TABLESPOONS CONFECTIONERS' SUGAR

$1/4$ TEASPOON VANILLA EXTRACT

2 TABLESPOONS LEMON JUICE

1 TABLESPOON FINELY GRATED LEMON RIND

1 EGG YOLK

$1 1/4$ CUPS ALL-PURPOSE FLOUR

$1/4$ CUP CORNSTARCH

$1/4$ TEASPOON BAKING POWDER

12 CANDIED CHERRIES, HALVED

GLAZE

2 TABLESPOONS LEMON JUICE

2 TABLESPOONS SUPERFINE SUGAR

MAKES ABOUT 20

◆ ◆ ◆

Cream the margarine with the confectioners' sugar until smooth. Add the vanilla extract, lemon juice and rind and egg yolk and beat again.

Sift together the flour, cornstarch and baking powder, add to the creamed mixture and work together to form a soft dough.

Put into a piping bag fitted with a $1/2$-inch star tip. Pipe about 20 shells onto greased baking sheets then place a half cherry on each. Bake at 350°F for 12-15 minutes.

Meanwhile, mix the lemon juice and superfine sugar together, brush over the cookies while still hot, then transfer to a wire rack to cool.

LEMON REFRIGERATOR COOKIES

The mixture for these cookies is chilled, then cut into thin slices before baking. It can also be stored uncooked in the refrigerator for a few days and used as required.

◆ ◆ ◆

$3/4$ CUP BUTTER

$1/2$ CUP SUPERFINE SUGAR

GRATED RIND OF 1 LEMON

1 EGG, BEATEN

$2 1/4$ CUPS ALL-PURPOSE FLOUR

SUPERFINE SUGAR AND GRATED NUTMEG TO DUST

MAKES 30

◆ ◆ ◆

Cream together the butter and sugar until very pale. Add the lemon rind and egg and beat until smooth. Stir in the flour and work together to a make a dough.

Turn onto a lightly floured work surface and knead until smooth. Form into 1 or 2 logs about $2 1/2$ inches in diameter. Wrap in waxed paper and refrigerate at least 1 hour or until firm.

Unwrap the dough and cut off thin cookies, placing them on greased baking sheets. Bake at 375°F for about 12 minutes until pale golden.

Dredge with superfine sugar and nutmeg while still warm. Leave to cool completely on a wire rack.

TOP: *Lemon Shells*
BOTTOM: *Lemon Refrigerator Cookies*

STRIPED CHOCOLATE AND VANILLA COOKIES

These butter cookies are made with chocolate and vanilla-flavored doughs which are layered and cut into strips.

◆ ◆ ◆

1 CUP BUTTER

1/2 CUP SUPERFINE SUGAR

2 1/2 CUPS ALL-PURPOSE FLOUR

2 TABLESPOONS UNSWEETENED COCOA

1 TEASPOON VANILLA EXTRACT

MAKES ABOUT 28

◆ ◆ ◆

Put the butter and sugar into a bowl and beat together until light and creamy. Add the flour and mix to make a dough. Transfer two-thirds of the dough to another bowl and work in the cocoa until evenly blended. Add the vanilla extract to the remaining piece of dough.

Roll out half of the chocolate dough to a rectangular strip 3 inches wide, 9 inches long and 1/2 inch thick. Place on a large sheet of waxed paper.

Roll out the vanilla dough to the same measurements, lightly brush the strips with water and place the vanilla on top of the chocolate.

Roll out the remaining chocolate dough and place on top of the vanilla. Wrap in the waxed paper and chill for at least 30 minutes.

Grease 2 baking sheets, unwrap the dough and with a sharp knife cut thin slices about 1/4 inch thick and place on the baking sheets. Bake at 350°F for 12-15 minutes. Cool for 2 minutes, then transfer to a wire rack.

COCONUT CRUNCHIES

Quick and easy to make, these cookies look good topped with shredded coconut before they are cooked.

◆ ◆ ◆

1 CUP SELF-RISING FLOUR

PINCH OF SALT

1 TEASPOON GROUND CINNAMON

1/2 CUP BUTTER OR MARGARINE

2/3 CUP SIFTED RAW SUGAR

1 EGG, BEATEN

1 CUP SHREDDED COCONUT

SHREDDED COCONUT TO DECORATE

MAKES 28-30

◆ ◆ ◆

Sift together the flour, salt and cinnamon. Cream the butter or margarine until light and fluffy, add the egg. Stir in flour and coconut until well blended.

Drop teaspoonfuls of the mixture onto greased baking sheets, allowing space for spreading, and flatten slightly with a fork. Top each one with a little shredded coconut. Bake at 350°F for 15-20 minutes until golden. Cool for a few moments, then transfer to a wire rack to cool completely.

TOP: *Coconut Crunchies*

BOTTOM: *Striped Chocolate and Vanilla Cookies*

CHOCOLATE ORANGE PINWEELS

These cookies look very impressive with their two-tone spirals. The prepared dough can be kept in the refrigerator for a few days and then cooked when needed.

◆ ◆ ◆

1 CUP BUTTER OR MARGARINE

$1/2$ CUP SUPERFINE SUGAR

$2^3/4$ CUPS ALL-PURPOSE FLOUR

1 TABLESPOON UNSWEETENED COCOA

2 TEASPOONS GRATED ORANGE RIND

MAKES ABOUT 36

◆ ◆ ◆

Cream the butter or margarine with the sugar until light and fluffy. Put half the mixture into another bowl and add $1^1/4$ cups of the flour and all the cocoa. Add the rest of the flour and the orange rind to the other half of the mixture.

Form both mixtures into smooth pliable doughs. Roll each one out to a rectangle, the same size, about 8 x 11 inch and $1/8$th inch thick.

Place the chocolate-flavored dough on a large piece of waxed paper, carefully place the orange dough on top. Roll up along the length like a jelly roll, using the waxed paper to guide the rolling. Wrap the roll in the paper.

Refrigerate the roll for at least 1 hour or until firm. Remove the paper and cut the dough in thin slices. Place the cookies on greased baking sheets and bake at 350°F for 10-15 minutes, or until golden. Cool for 2 minutes, then transfer to a wire rack to cool completely.

GINGER SNAPS

These are sometimes called Ginger Nuts, probably because they are hard, but still delicious to eat.

◆ ◆ ◆

$2^1/4$ CUPS ALL-PURPOSE FLOUR

1 TEASPOON BAKING OF SODA

1 TABLESPOON GROUND GINGER

$1/2$ TEASPOON ALLSPICE

$1/3$ CUP BUTTER

$2/3$ CUP SIFTED RAW SUGAR

3 TABLESPOONS LIGHT CORN SYRUP

1 EGG, BEATEN

MAKES ABOUT 36

◆ ◆ ◆

Sift together the flour, baking soda, ginger and allspice. Set aside.

Beat the butter with the sugar and light corn syrup until creamy, add the egg and beat again.

Stir in the dry ingredients and mix to form a firm and pliable dough. Take pieces of the dough about the size of a small walnut and roll each in the palm of the hand to make a ball.

Place the balls on greased baking sheets and flatten slightly. Bake at 325°F for 15-20 minutes, until firm. The tops should have small cracks on the surface. Cool for a few moments, then transfer to a wire rack to cool completely.

TOP: *Chocolate Orange Pinwheels*
BOTTOM: *Ginger Snaps*

ANZACS

Originally from Australia, these cookies are now famous all over the world and a favorite of many families.

◆ ◆ ◆

1 CUP ROLLED OATS

1 1/4 CUPS WHOLEWHEAT FLOUR

1 CUP SHREDDED COCONUT

1/2 CUP GOLDEN SUPERFINE SUGAR

2 TABLESPOONS LIGHT CORN SYRUP

2/3 CUP SUNFLOWER MARGARINE

3 TABLESPOONS WATER

1 1/2 TEASPOONS BAKING SODA

MAKES ABOUT 30

◆ ◆ ◆

Put the oats, flour, coconut and sugar into a bowl and mix together.

Put the light corn syrup, margarine and water into a pan and heat until boiling. Immediately add the baking soda, allow it to foam up, then add to the dry ingredients and mix together.

Place spoonfuls of the mixture onto greased baking sheets and bake at 325°F for 12-15 minutes until a rich golden color.

Cool slightly, then transfer to a wire rack to cool completely.

ALMOND CRISPS

A light and crisp cookie which will keep well in an airtight container for a few days.

◆ ◆ ◆

1/2 CUP UNSALTED BUTTER

1/3 CUP SUPERFINE SUGAR

1 LARGE EGG YOLK

FEW DROPS OF ALMOND EXTRACT

1/2 CUP BLANCHED ALMONDS, LIGHTLY

TOASTED

1 1/4 CUPS SELF-RISING FLOUR

SUPERFINE SUGAR TO DECORATE

MAKES 24

◆ ◆ ◆

Cream together the butter and sugar until light and fluffy, add the egg yolk and almond extract and mix well.

Chop the almonds (not too finely) and add to the mixture with the flour. Mix together to make a dough.

Form into 24 balls and place on greased baking sheets. Take a heavy-bottomed glass, dip in superfine sugar and press down each ball to flatten, dipping the glass in sugar each time.

Bake the cookies at 350°F for 12-15 minutes. Cool for 1 minute, then transfer to a rack to cool completely.

TOP: *Anzacs*
BOTTOM: *Almond Crisps*

GINGERBREAD FOLK

*Children of all ages will love to help
make and decorate these favorite cookies.*

◆ ◆ ◆

4 CUPS ALL-PURPOSE FLOUR

1 TABLESPOON GROUND GINGER

1 TEASPOON APPLE PIE SPICE

2 TEASPOONS BAKING SODA

1/2 CUP BUTTER OR MARGARINE

1/4 CUP LIGHT CORN SYRUP

2/3 CUP RAW SUGAR

1 EGG, BEATEN

CURRANTS

CANDIED CHERRIES (OPTIONAL)

1/2 CUP CONFECTIONERS' SUGAR

MAKES ABOUT 40

◆ ◆ ◆

Sift the flour into a bowl with the spices and baking soda. Put the butter or margarine into a saucepan with the syrup and raw sugar, heat gently until melted. Pour onto the dry ingredients, add the egg and mix together to make a dough. The dough will look sticky to begin with, but will become more elastic and firm as it cools.

Roll out to about 1/8 th inch thick and cut out with gingerbread people shapes. Transfer to greased baking sheets and add currants for eyes and pieces of candied cherries for mouth if wished.

Bake at 325°F for 15-18 minutes. Remove from trays and transfer to wire racks to cool.

Mix the confectioners' sugar with 3-4 teaspoons water to make a thick consistency. Pipe buttons, bows etc on the cooled cookies.

VANILLA SUGAR COOKIES

*Cut these cookies into any shape you wish.
For a children's party, try some novelty or
animal shapes.*

◆ ◆ ◆

1/2 CUP BUTTER OR MARGARINE

1 1/4 CUPS ALL-PURPOSE FLOUR

1/4 CUP CORNSTARCH

1/4 CUP VANILLA-FLAVORED SUGAR

1 TEASPOON VANILLA EXTRACT

2/3 CUP CONFECTIONERS' SUGAR

SUGAR STRANDS OR COLORED SUGAR

CRYSTALS

**MAKES ABOUT 18-28
DEPENDING ON SIZE OF CUTTERS**

◆ ◆ ◆

Rub the butter or margarine into the flours until the mixture resembles fine breadcrumbs. Add the vanilla-flavored sugar and extract and work together to make a firm dough. Lightly knead until smooth, wrap and chill for 1 hour until firm.

Roll out the dough, not too thinly, and cut into chosen shapes. If using sugar crystals, brush the cookies with egg white and sprinkle over the sugar. Place on greased baking sheets and bake at 350°F for 10-12 minutes. Allow to cool for 1 minute, then lift onto a wire rack to cool completely.

Mix the confectioners' sugar with a little water to make a thick mixture, place a small teaspoonful on each cookie and spread evenly. Decorate with sugar strands.

TOP: *Gingerbread Folk*
BOTTOM: *Vanilla Sugar Cookies*

ITALIAN BUTTER COOKIES

This recipe uses a cookie press, a marvelous invention for making different shaped cookies, just by changing the cutting disc. Once mastered, two different colored doughs can be placed in the tube to give some interesting effects. The dough can also be rolled out and cut with small cookie cutters.

◆ ◆ ◆

$3/4$ CUP UNSALTED BUTTER

$1/3$ CUP SUPERFINE SUGAR

FEW DROPS OF ALMOND EXTRACT

1 EGG YOLK

$2 1/4$ CUPS ALL-PURPOSE FLOUR

SUPERFINE OR CONFECTIONERS' SUGAR TO DUST

MAKES ABOUT 50

◆ ◆ ◆

Cream together the butter and sugar until light and fluffy. Add the almond extract, then gradually add the flour to make a firm dough.

Take about a quarter of the dough and knead lightly, form into a log shape and place inside the cylinder of the cookie press. Attach the desired shape cutter and press out onto greased baking sheets.

Bake at 375°F for 10-12 minutes or until lightly browned. Transfer to wire racks to cool and sprinkle with superfine sugar while warm, or with confectioners' sugar when cold.

COCONUT MACAROONS

An unusual recipe for macaroons, the addition of almond paste gives these cookies a scrumptious flavor.

◆ ◆ ◆

4 OUNCES ALMOND PASTE

$1/3$ CUP SUPERFINE SUGAR

$1 1/4$ CUPS SHREDDED COCONUT

3 EGG WHITES

5 CANDIED CHERRIES, QUARTERED

MAKES ABOUT 20

◆ ◆ ◆

Put the almond paste into a food processor with the sugar and work together until the mixture resembles fine crumbs.

Whisk the egg whites until stiff, carefully fold in the almond paste crumbs and the coconut. Drop spoonfuls in heaped mounds onto baking sheets lined with either rice paper or non-stick baking parchment paper.

Place a quartered cherry on each and bake at 300°F for about 25 minutes until golden.

If using rice paper break it off around each cookie, if using parchment paper, the macaroons will peel off easily. Cool on a wire rack. Store in an airtight container for up to a week. Do not freeze.

TOP: *Italian Butter Cookies*
BOTTOM: *Coconut Macaroons*

OATY SHORTBREAD

*There are many recipes for shortbread.
This one, which is quite crunchy, is
delicious to have with iced tea.*

◆ ◆ ◆

³/₄ CUP UNSALTED BUTTER

¹/₃ CUP GOLDEN SUPERFINE SUGAR

1 CUP ALL-PURPOSE FLOUR

PINCH OF SALT

1 TEASPOON GROUND CINNAMON

1 CUP ROLLED OATS

SUGAR TO DUST

MAKES 12 PIECES

◆ ◆ ◆

Beat the butter and sugar together until light and
creamy. In another bowl mix the dry ingredients together, then add to the creamy mixture. The texture will be
crumbly and loose. Turn into an ungreased 9-inch
loose-bottomed pie pan. Dip fingers in a little extra
rolled oats and press the mixture evenly into the pan.

Smooth the top and prick all over with a fork. Bake
the shortbread at 350°F for about 40 minutes. While
still warm, take a sharp knife and score the shortbread
into 12 wedges. Sprinkle the top with sugar and leave
to cool in the pan. When cold the shortbread can be
cut into portions.

OATMEAL RAISIN COOKIES

*These wholesome cookies, which use
high-fiber ingredients, would make a healthy
addition to packed lunches and picnics.*

◆ ◆ ◆

¹/₂ CUP SUNFLOWER MARGARINE

¹/₂ CUP MEDIUM OATMEAL

1 ¹/₂ CUPS WHOLEWHEAT FLOUR

1 TEASPOON GROUND CINNAMON

¹/₃ CUP GOLDEN GRANULATED SUGAR

²/₃ CUP RAISINS

1 LARGE EGG, BEATEN

A LITTLE MILK

MAKES 20

◆ ◆ ◆

Put the margarine into a bowl with the oatmeal and
flour and rub together to form a crumbly mixture.

Stir in the cinnamon, sugar and raisins, then mix
together with the egg and a little milk to make a firm
dough.

Form into 20 balls and place on greased baking sheets.
Press down with a fork and bake at 350°F for 15-20
minutes until firm to the touch.

Allow to cool slightly, then transfer to a wire rack to
cool completely.

TOP: *Oaty Shortbread*
BOTTOM: *Oatmeal Raisin Cookies*

APRICOT SABLES

These sables (meaning sand) are the French version of a Scottish shortbread. They should be light and crumbly.

◆ ◆ ◆

2 CUPS ALL-PURPOSE FLOUR

²/₃ CUP CONFECTIONERS' SUGAR

³/₄ CUP UNSALTED BUTTER

¹/₂ CUP GROUND ALMONDS

¹/₃ CUP FINELY CHOPPED READY-TO-EAT
DRIED APRICOTS

1 LARGE EGG YOLK

1 TABLESPOON APRICOT CONSERVE

MAKES ABOUT 30

◆ ◆ ◆

Sift the flour and confectioners' sugar into a bowl. Rub in the butter until the mixture resembles fine crumbs. Stir in the ground almonds and apricots, then bind together with the egg yolk.

Lightly knead the dough on a barely floured surface until smooth, then wrap in plastic wrap and chill in the refrigerator for 1 hour.

Roll out the dough to a thickness of ¹/₄ inch and cut out cookies with a glass or cookie cutter 2 inches in diameter. Place on greased baking sheets and refrigerate for 30 minutes.

Put the apricot conserve into a small parchment paper piping bag and pipe a small blob on each biscuit. Bake at 325°F for 15-20 minutes until pale golden. Cool slightly, then transfer to a rack to cool completely.

HONEY JUMBLES

These are sometimes known as Bosworth Jumbles. The story goes that the recipe was dropped by King Richard's cook on the battlefield of Bosworth.

◆ ◆ ◆

²/₃ CUP BUTTER

¹/₄ CUP GOLDEN SUPERFINE SUGAR

3 TABLESPOONS CLEAR HONEY

1 EGG, BEATEN

2¹/₂ CUPS ALL-PURPOSE FLOUR

¹/₂ CUP GROUND ALMONDS

2 TABLESPOONS CLEAR HONEY, WARMED

GOLDEN SUPERFINE SUGAR TO DUST

MAKES ABOUT 24

◆ ◆ ◆

Cream the butter, sugar and honey together until light and pale. Gradually work in the egg, flour and ground almonds.

Work the mixture into a dough. Take small pieces of dough and roll each into a smooth ball, then into a sausage shape 4 inches long. Form into 'S' shapes and carefully place on greased baking sheets.

Bake at 350°F for 10-12 minutes until golden. Brush with the warmed honey and sprinkle with sugar. Lift off and cool on a wire rack.

TOP: *Honey Jumbles*
BOTTOM: *Apricot Sables*

HAZELNUT DOLLARS

Toasting the hazelnuts really helps to bring out the flavor in these cookies. Some supermarkets sell hazelnuts ready chopped.

◆ ◆ ◆

$^2/_3$ CUP UNSALTED BUTTER

$^1/_3$ CUP SUPERFINE SUGAR

1 TEASPOON VANILLA EXTRACT

$1^1/_2$ CUPS ALL-PURPOSE FLOUR

$^1/_2$ TEASPOON BAKING POWDER

$^1/_2$ CUP LIGHTLY TOASTED, FINELY CHOPPED HAZELNUTS

2 SQUARES DARK CHOCOLATE

MAKES ABOUT 24

◆ ◆ ◆

Beat the butter and sugar together until light and creamy. Add the vanilla extract. Sift the flour with the baking powder and mix into the creamed mixture with the nuts.

Work together to make a dough and knead lightly on a floured surface until smooth. Wrap in plastic wrap and chill for 1 hour.

Roll out thinly and cut into rounds with a 3-inch fluted cutter. Carefully place the cookies on greased baking sheets and bake at 375°F for 6-8 minutes.

Cool slightly, then transfer to a wire rack to cool completely. Melt the chocolate and allow to cool. Place in a small parchment paper piping bag and drizzle over the cookies. Leave to set.

DUTCH SHORTCAKES

A classic cookie mixture which can be piped in different shapes. Rich in flavor and crumbly in texture, these shortcakes make a lovely gift presented in an attractive tin or box.

◆ ◆ ◆

1 CUP SOFTENED UNSALTED BUTTER

$^1/_3$ CUP SUPERFINE SUGAR

$^1/_2$ TEASPOON VANILLA EXTRACT

2 CUPS ALL-PURPOSE FLOUR

$^1/_2$ CUP CORNSTARCH

SUPERFINE OR CONFECTIONERS' SUGAR TO DUST

MAKES ABOUT 24-27

◆ ◆ ◆

Beat the butter and sugar together until very light and creamy. Add the vanilla extract.

Sift the flour and cornstarch together, then add to the creamed mixture and mix to make a soft dough.

Put the dough into a piping bag fitted with a large star tip and pipe out whirls or 'S' shapes onto greased baking sheets.

Bake at 350°F for 15-20 minutes until very lightly golden. Transfer to a rack to cool. Either sprinkle with superfine sugar while warm or dust with confectioners' sugar when cool.

TOP: *Dutch Shortcakes*
BOTTOM: *Hazelnut Dollars*

CHOCOLATE CHUNK AND NUT COOKIES

*The combination of chocolate
and nuts in these melt-in-the-mouth cookies
is quite irresistible.*

◆ ◆ ◆

$^1/_2$ CUP BUTTER

$^1/_2$ CUP GRANULATED SUGAR

$^1/_2$ CUP SIFTED RAW SUGAR

2 EGGS, BEATEN

2 TEASPOONS VANILLA EXTRACT

$2^1/_4$ CUPS ALL-PURPOSE FLOUR, SIFTED

1 TEASPOON BAKING POWDER

4 SQUARES DARK CHOCOLATE,

CUT INTO SMALL CHUNKS

1 CUP ROUGHLY CHOPPED HAZELNUTS

MAKES 16

◆ ◆ ◆

In a bowl cream together the butter and sugars until light in consistency. Beat in the eggs and vanilla extract. Sift in the flour and baking powder and stir in the chocolate and nuts.

Place dessert spoonfuls on greased baking sheets and flatten slightly. Bake at 350°F for 10-12 minutes.

Cool for 2 minutes, then transfer to a wire rack to cool completely.

MELTING MOMENTS

*Children love to make these cookies,
probably because they are easy to prepare,
but more because they are so good to eat.*

◆ ◆ ◆

$^1/_2$ CUP BUTTER

$^1/_3$ CUP SUPERFINE SUGAR

1 EGG YOLK

1 TEASPOON VANILLA EXTRACT

$1^1/_4$ CUPS SELF-RISING FLOUR

1 CUP CORNFLAKES

10 CANDIED CHERRIES, HALVED

MAKES 20

◆ ◆ ◆

Cream together the butter and sugar, beat in the egg yolk and vanilla extract. Gradually work in the flour to make a soft dough. Chill for 30 minutes.

Divide the mixture into 20 balls. Crush the cornflakes slightly and place on a plate. Take each ball and gently press one side onto the cornflakes, flattening them a little. Place on greased baking sheets, cornflake side up, and place a half cherry in the center of each biscuit.

Bake at 375°F for 15-20 minutes until golden-brown. Cool for 2-3 minutes, then transfer to a wire rack to cool completely.

TOP: *Chocolate Chunk and Nut Cookies*
BOTTOM: *Melting Moments*

JELLY-FILLED BUTTER COOKIES

Cut these cookies in any shape, depending on the cutters available – even plain round cookies will look good.

◆ ◆ ◆

2 CUPS ALL-PURPOSE FLOUR

$1/_2$ CUP CONFECTIONERS' SUGAR

$1/_2$ TEASPOON BAKING POWDER

$1/_2$ CUP BUTTER

1 EGG YOLK

$1/_2$ TEASPOON VANILLA EXTRACT

STRAWBERRY OR RASPBERRY JELLY

CONFECTIONERS' SUGAR TO DUST

MAKES ABOUT 16

◆ ◆ ◆

Put the flour, confectioners' sugar and baking powder into a bowl, add the butter and rub in to resemble fine crumbs. Mix to a dough with the egg yolk and extract. Knead until smooth, then wrap in plastic wrap and refrigerate for 1 hour until firm.

Roll out thinly and use a 2-3-inch diameter cutter to cut out the cookies. Place on greased baking sheets. Cut the centers out of half of the cookies with a small round or shaped cutter.

Bake at 375°F for 8-10 minutes or until light golden in color. Cool for a few moments, then transfer to a wire rack to cool competely.

When cold, spread jelly on the whole cookies, top with the other cookies and dust with confectioners' sugar.

PEANUT CRUNCHIES

Peanuts are an all-time favorite with many families. Quick and easy to make, these cookies can always have a place in the cookie jar.

◆ ◆ ◆

$1/_2$ CUP BUTTER

$1/_2$ CUP CRUNCHY PEANUT BUTTER

$2/_3$ CUP SIFTED RAW SUGAR

$2/_3$ CUP CONFECTIONERS' SUGAR

1 LARGE EGG, BEATEN

$1/_2$ TEASPOON VANILLA EXTRACT

2 CUPS ALL-PURPOSE FLOUR

1 TEASPOON BAKING POWDER

$3/_4$ CUP ROUGHLY CHOPPED PEANUT KERNELS

MAKES ABOUT 30

◆ ◆ ◆

Put the butter into a bowl with the peanut butter and both sugars, beat together well. Add the egg and vanilla extract and beat again.

Sift together the flour and baking powder, add to the creamed mixture and mix until well blended. Take heaped teaspoonfuls of the mixture and roll into balls. Press each onto the chopped nuts, flattening down slightly at the same time.

Place the cookies on greased baking sheets, then bake at 350°F for 10-12 minutes. Cool for 2 minutes, then transfer the cookies to a wire rack to cool completely.

TOP: *Peanut Crunchies*
BOTTOM: *Jelly-filled Butter Cookies*

LUXURY TREATS

With the addition of other ingredients, such as candied cherries, almond paste, dried fruit and nuts, simple basic recipes can be turned into very special cookies, and using unusual shaped cutters and sandwiching layers together adds an extra touch of luxury. The cookies in this chapter are ideal for special occasions and many of them make delicious accompaniments to fruit mousses, sorbets and ice-creams. They also make delightful gifts, wrapped in pretty paper or presented as a selection arranged in a basket.

Most cookie recipes only require basic kitchen equipment; always use measuring spoons and cups for accurate weighing. The most important item is the baking sheet. For even baking and browning, a strong aluminum sheet gives excellent results. It is worth having more than one baking sheet, as it is much easier to spoon and shape the mixture all at once and cook at the same time. Use melted butter for greasing, but do not overgrease or the cookies will become too dark underneath. Non-stick baking parchment is essential to prevent rich doughs and meringues from sticking to baking sheets. It is also useful when rolling out a mixture that is difficult to handle – just place the dough between two sheets of the paper.

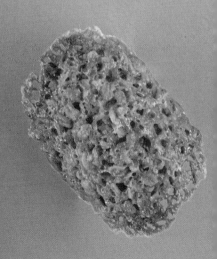

CONTENTS

◆ ◆ ◆

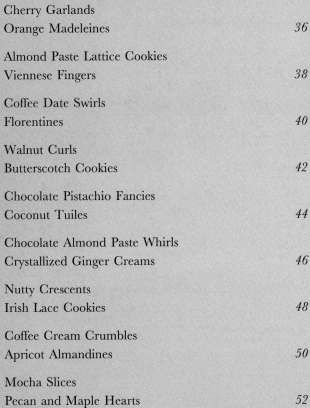

CHERRY GARLANDS

An attractive cookie, which has a slightly fragrant rosewater glaze.

❖ ❖ ❖

2 CUPS ALL-PURPOSE FLOUR

²/₃ CUP BUTTER

¹/₂ CUP SUPERFINE SUGAR

¹/₂ TEASPOON VANILLA EXTRACT

1 EGG, BEATEN

²/₃ CUP FINELY CHOPPED CHERRIES

¹/₂ CUP CONFECTIONERS' SUGAR

1 TABLESPOON ROSEWATER

4-5 TEASPOONS WATER

CANDIED CHERRIES

MAKES 24

❖ ❖ ❖

Sift the flour into a bowl, add the butter and rub in until the mixture has a fine texture. Add the sugar. Stir in the extract with the egg and cherries and mix together to make a firm dough.

Knead lightly then take small pieces of dough and roll them into balls the size of a large pea. Arrange 8 balls in rings on greased baking sheets, pressing together slightly. Continue making rings until all the dough is used up. Bake at 375°F for 12-15 minutes. Cool for 2 minutes, then transfer to a wire rack to cool completely.

Sift the confectioners' sugar into a bowl, add the rosewater and enough water to make a smooth runny glaze. Dip the tops of the cookies into the glaze then decorate each one with small pieces of cherry.

ORANGE MADELEINE COOKIES

A madeleine pan is ideal for this recipe, but if you don't have one, you can use a small-holed muffin pan instead.

❖ ❖ ❖

³/₄ CUP UNSALTED BUTTER

¹/₃ CUP SUGAR

3 TEASPOONS GRATED ORANGE RIND

1¹/₄ CUPS ALL-PURPOSE FLOUR

¹/₂ CUP GROUND ALMONDS

¹/₂ CUP CORNSTARCH

SUPERFINE SUGAR TO DUST

MAKES ABOUT 20

❖ ❖ ❖

Put the butter and sugar into a bowl and beat together until light and fluffy. Add the orange rind, then sift in the flour, almonds and cornstarch and mix together to form a soft paste.

The mixture may have to be cooked in two batches, depending on the size of the pan.

Press a little of the mixture into the well greased and floured molds of the madeleine pan and smooth off the tops. Bake at 350°F for 15-20 minutes. Cool the cookies a little before carefully easing them out of the pan. Place on a wire rack, sprinkle with sugar and leave to cool completely.

TOP: *Orange Madeleine Cookies*
BOTTOM: *Cherry Garlands*

ALMOND PASTE LATTICE COOKIES

For lovers of almond paste these sandwiched cookies will be a real treat.

◆ ◆ ◆

2 CUPS ALL-PURPOSE FLOUR

1/2 TEASPOON BAKING POWDER

3/4 CUP UNSALTED BUTTER

1/2 CUP SUPERFINE SUGAR

1 EGG YOLK

8 OUNCES ALMOND PASTE

3 TABLESPOONS APRICOT CONSERVE

3/4 CUP CONFECTIONERS' SUGAR

YELLOW FOOD COLORING

MAKES 20

◆ ◆ ◆

Sift the flour and baking powder into a bowl, add the butter and rub in until the mixture has a fine texture. Add the sugar and mix to a dough with the egg yolk. Knead lightly until smooth, then wrap and chill.

Roll out the dough thinly, then cut into rounds or ovals about 3 inches in diameter and place on greased baking sheets. Bake at 325°F for 15 minutes. Transfer to a wire rack to cool.

Roll out the almond paste thinly and cut out rounds or ovals the same size as the cookies. Spread half the cookies with conserve, place almond paste on top, then spread with a little more conserve and sandwich with the remaining cookies.

Sift the confectioners' sugar into a bowl and mix with a little water and a few drops of yellow food coloring to make a thick glaze. Place in a small parchment paper piping bag and decorate each cookie. Allow to set.

VIENNESE FINGERS

An all-time favorite, these delicious cookies are finished with chocolate. For a less rich cookie, omit the chocolate and dust with confectioners' sugar.

◆ ◆ ◆

1 CUP SOFTENED UNSALTED BUTTER

6 TABLESPOONS CONFECTIONERS' SUGAR

2 TEASPOONS VANILLA EXTRACT

1 LARGE EGG, BEATEN

2 1/2 CUPS ALL-PURPOSE FLOUR

1/2 TEASPOON BAKING POWDER

8 SQUARES DARK CHOCOLATE

MAKES ABOUT 28

◆ ◆ ◆

Put the butter into a bowl with the confectioners' sugar and beat together until pale and soft. Beat in the vanilla extract and egg. Sift in the flour and baking powder, and mix together to make a smooth dough.

Place the mixture in a piping bag fitted with a medium star tip and pipe finger shapes about 3 inches long onto greased baking sheets. Bake at 375°F for 15-20 minutes until crisp and pale golden. Transfer to a wire rack to cool.

To make the frosting, break the chocolate into a bowl. Stand the bowl over a pan of simmering water and stir until the chocolate has melted.

Dip both ends of the cookies in the chocolate, then leave on a wire rack to set.

TOP: *Almond Paste Lattice Cookies*
BOTTOM: *Viennese Fingers*

COFFEE DATE SWIRLS

Delicious served with coffee after dinner.

◆ ◆ ◆

$^3/_4$ CUP UNSALTED BUTTER

$^1/_4$ CUP GOLDEN SUPERFINE SUGAR

1 TABLESPOON INSTANT COFFEE DISSOLVED IN

1 TEASPOON HOT WATER

1 EGG, BEATEN

2 CUPS ALL-PURPOSE FLOUR

FILLING

$1^1/_2$ CUPS CHOPPED PITTED DATES

$^2/_3$ CUP WATER

1 TABLESPOON DARK RUM

$^1/_2$ CUP GROUND ALMONDS

M A K E S   A B O U T   3 6

◆ ◆ ◆

Put the butter and sugar into a bowl and beat together until pale and creamy. Add the dissolved coffee to the mixture with the egg and beat again. Sift in the flour, then work together to make a stiff dough. Knead lightly until smooth, then wrap and chill.

To make the filling, put the dates into a saucepan with the water and simmer for about 10 minutes until the dates are soft and the water has evaporated. Allow to cool, then mash with a fork. Stir in the rum and ground almonds.

Roll out the dough to a rectangle about 9 x 13 inches. Spread over the date mixture, then roll up along the long side, jelly-roll style. Wrap and chill until firm.

Cut $^1/_4$-inch slices and place on baking sheets lined with non-stick baking parchment paper. Bake at 350°F for 12-15 minutes.

FLORENTINES

Florentines are a rich mixture of nuts and fruits, coated on one side with chocolate.

◆ ◆ ◆

$^1/_4$ CUP BUTTER

$^1/_3$ CUP SUPERFINE SUGAR

$^1/_2$ CUP COARSELY CHOPPED

BLANCHED ALMONDS

$^1/_4$ CUP CHOPPED HAZELNUTS

2 TABLESPOONS FINELY CHOPPED

CRYSTALLIZED GINGER

$^1/_3$ CUP CHOPPED CHERRIES

$^1/_3$ CUP MIXED PEEL

$^1/_4$ CUP ALL-PURPOSE FLOUR

3 TABLESPOONS LIGHT CREAM

6 SQUARES DARK CHOCOLATE

M A K E S   A B O U T   2 0

◆ ◆ ◆

Melt the butter in a saucepan, then stir in the sugar and continue to stir over the heat until dissolved. Add the remaining ingredients except the chocolate.

Place dessert spoonfuls of the mixture onto greased baking sheets and flatten. Bake at 350°F for 10 minutes until golden. Use a palette knife and push in the ragged edges to neaten. Cool for 2 minutes, then transfer to wire racks to cool completely.

Melt the chocolate in a bowl over a pan of simmering water. Spread over the undersides of the florentines. Allow the chocolate to set a little, then make a wavy pattern with a fork. Leave to set.

TOP: *Florentines*
BOTTOM: *Coffee Date Swirls*

WALNUT CURLS

Although these cookies are a bit fiddly to make, the mixture is simple and the result is elegant.

◆ ◆ ◆

$1/4$ CUP BUTTER

$1/2$ CUP SUPERFINE SUGAR

2 EGG WHITES

$1/3$ CUP ALL-PURPOSE FLOUR

$1/2$ CUP VERY FINELY CHOPPED WALNUTS

MAKES 21

◆ ◆ ◆

Put the butter and sugar into a bowl and beat until light and creamy. Add the egg whites and beat until well combined but not frothy. Sift in the flour and fold it in with the nuts.

Drop teaspoonfuls of the mixture onto baking sheets lined with non-stick baking parchment paper and spread the batter into 2-inch rounds. Bake at 350°F for 5-6 minutes, or until just turning golden round the edges.

Working quickly with each cookie, remove from the paper with a flat fish slice or palette knife, and roll, with the underside of the cookie inside, around pencils or chopsticks. Transfer to a wire rack to cool. If the cookies become too brittle to roll, return them to the oven for 30 seconds to soften.

BUTTERSCOTCH COOKIES

Topping these cookies with broken butterscotch candies gives an interesting finish and delicious taste.

◆ ◆ ◆

$1/2$ CUP SOFT MARGARINE

$1/2$ TEASPOON VANILLA EXTRACT

4 TABLESPOONS SIFTED RAW SUGAR

$1 1/4$ CUPS ALL-PURPOSE FLOUR

$1/4$ CUP CUSTARD POWDER

$1/3$ CUP ROUGHLY CRUSHED

BUTTERSCOTCH CANDIES

MAKES 15

◆ ◆ ◆

Beat the margarine and sugar together until fluffy, add the vanilla extract, then sift in the flour and mix to form a soft dough. Spoon into a piping bag fitted with a large star tip.

Pipe swirls onto greased baking sheets and top with the crushed butterscotch. Chill for 30 minutes.

Bake at 375°F for 10-12 minutes until pale golden. Cool slightly, then transfer to a wire rack to cool completely.

TOP: *Walnut Curls*
BOTTOM: *Butterscotch Cookies*

CHOCOLATE PISTACHIO FANCIES

Buy ready shelled pistachios for this recipe and make sure they are unsalted. The combination of the nuts and chocolate make these cookies a special treat.

◆ ◆ ◆

$^2/_3$ CUP BUTTER

$^1/_2$ TEASPOON VANILLA EXTRACT

$^1/_2$ CUP SIFTED RAW SUGAR

$^3/_4$ CUP CHOPPED PISTACHIOS

$1^1/_4$ CUPS ALL-PURPOSE FLOUR

3 TABLESPOONS UNSWEETENED COCOA

TOPPING

5 SQUARES GERMAN SWEET CHOCOLATE

2 TABLESPOONS UNSALTED BUTTER

$^1/_2$ CUP CHOPPED PISTACHIOS

MAKES 18

◆ ◆ ◆

Put the butter, vanilla extract and sugar into a bowl and beat until creamy. Add the nuts and sift in the flour and cocoa. Mix together to form a fairly stiff consistency.

Line a 9-inch shallow square baking pan with non-stick baking parchment paper, then add the mixture. Flatten out evenly and bake at 375°F for 12-15 minutes. Allow to cool in the pan.

To make the topping, put the chocolate and butter into a bowl and place over a pan of simmering water. Stir until melted, then spread over the cookie base. Scatter over the chopped nuts and allow to set.

Cut into 9 squares, then cut each square diagonally to give 18 triangles. Remove from the tin.

COCONUT TUILES

A simple mixture made to look impressive by curling the cookies while still warm.

◆ ◆ ◆

2 EGG WHITES

$^1/_2$ CUP SUPERFINE SUGAR

$^1/_4$ CUP MELTED UNSALTED BUTTER

$^1/_2$ CUP ALL-PURPOSE FLOUR

1 CUP SHREDDED COCONUT

MAKES ABOUT 18

◆ ◆ ◆

Whisk the egg whites until very frothy, fold in the sugar, then the melted butter. Sift in the flour and add half the coconut. Use a large metal spoon to mix the ingredients together.

Line 2 baking sheets with non-stick baking parchment paper. Spread dessert spoonfuls of the mixture onto the paper to form circles about 3 inches in diameter. Sprinkle each with some of the remaining coconut and bake at 375°F for 5-6 minutes until golden.

Loosen the edges with a palette knife and lift each off with a spatula. Place on a rolling pin and leave to cool. Do not cook too many at a time, otherwise it will be difficult to shape them.

The non-stick paper can be turned and re-used to bake more cookies.

TOP: *Coconut Tuiles*
BOTTOM: *Chocolate Pistachio Fancies*

CHOCOLATE ALMOND PASTE WHIRLS

An indulgent treat, these almond paste-flavored cookies are topped with a rich chocolate ganache. For extra flavor add a little amaretto liqueur to the topping mixture.

◆ ◆ ◆

$^1/_2$ CUP UNSALTED BUTTER

4 OUNCES ALMOND PASTE

FEW DROPS OF ALMOND EXTRACT

1$^1/_2$ CUPS ALL-PURPOSE FLOUR

TOPPING

$^2/_3$ CUP HEAVY CREAM

10 SQUARES DARK CHOCOLATE

BLANCHED ALMONDS

MAKES ABOUT 24

◆ ◆ ◆

Put the butter and almond paste into a bowl and beat together until creamy. Add the almond extract and the flour, then work together to make a smooth dough. Knead lightly, then roll out to $^1/_4$ inch thick.

Use a 2-inch cutter and cut out rounds, place them on greased baking sheets and chill for 30 minutes. Bake at 350°F for 10-12 minutes until golden. Transfer to a wire rack to cool.

Meanwhile, put the cream into a pan and heat to boiling point, remove from the heat and add the broken up chocolate. Stir until the chocolate melts and is smooth. Allow to cool, then refrigerate until the mixture becomes thick enough to pipe.

Put the chocolate into a piping bag fitted with a star tip and pipe whirls on top of the biscuits. Decorate each cookie with a blanched almond.

CRYSTALLIZED GINGER CREAMS

The filling for these cookies uses crystallized ginger. If this is not available use stem ginger drained from its syrup or alternatively ginger marmalade.

◆ ◆ ◆

$^3/_4$ CUP UNSALTED BUTTER

5 TABLESPOONS CONFECTIONERS' SUGAR

1$^1/_2$ CUPS ALL-PURPOSE FLOUR

$^1/_2$ CUP CUSTARD POWDER

2 TEASPOONS GROUND GINGER

FILLING

$^1/_2$ CUP CONFECTIONERS' SUGAR

2 TABLESPOONS BUTTER

1$^1/_2$ TABLESPOONS FINELY CHOPPED CRYSTALLIZED OR CANDIED GINGER

MAKES 16-18

◆ ◆ ◆

Put the butter and confectioners' sugar into a bowl and beat together until creamy. Sift the flour with the custard powder and ginger, and mix in to make a stiff dough.

Take pieces of the mixture and form into balls the size of a large walnut. Place on greased baking sheets, press down and flatten with a fork. Bake at 350°F for 10-12 minutes until golden. Transfer to a wire rack to cool.

To make the filling, put the confectioners' sugar and butter into a bowl and beat together until creamy. Add the ginger and use to sandwich the cookies together.

TOP: *Chocolate Almond Paste Whirls*
BOTTOM: *Crystallized Ginger Creams*

NUTTY CRESCENTS

Many countries have recipes for crescent-shaped butter cookies with ground nuts and sugar. The Greeks have Kourambiedes and the Viennese Kupferlin.

◆ ◆ ◆

1 CUP UNSALTED BUTTER

$^1/_2$ CUP SUPERFINE SUGAR

$2^1/_2$ CUPS ALL-PURPOSE FLOUR

$1^3/_4$ CUPS LIGHTLY TOASTED HAZELNUTS,
GROUND

$^1/_2$ TEASPOON VANILLA EXTRACT

CONFECTIONERS' SUGAR TO DUST

M A K E S   A B O U T   3 0

◆ ◆ ◆

Put the butter into a bowl with the sugar and sift in the flour. Rub in until the mixture resembles very fine crumbs. Add the nuts and vanilla extract and mix together until the dough is smooth.

Take small pieces of dough and roll into 4-inch lengths. Shape into small crescents and place on greased baking sheets. Bake at 350°F for 10-15 minutes until golden.

Transfer to a wire rack to cool, then dust liberally with confectioners' sugar.

IRISH LACE COOKIES

These attractive cookies are quite delicate and require careful handling.

◆ ◆ ◆

$^1/_2$ CUP BUTTER

$^1/_2$ CUP SIFTED RAW SUGAR

2 TABLESPOONS LIGHT CORN SYRUP

$^1/_4$ CUP ALL-PURPOSE FLOUR

1 CUP ROLLED OATS

1 TEASPOON VANILLA EXTRACT

2 TABLESPOONS MILK

M A K E S   2 5

◆ ◆ ◆

Melt the butter in a saucepan, then stir in the sugar and corn syrup. Add the remaining ingredients and mix again. Drop rounded teaspoons of the mixture onto greased baking sheets and bake at 350°F for 8-9 minutes until golden-brown.

Cool for just 1 minute, then carefully remove with a spatula and place on a rolling pin to cool. If the cookies become brittle, return them to the oven for 30 seconds to soften. Do not cook too many at once, otherwise it will be difficult to shape them. Once the cookies have cooled in shape, transfer them to a wire rack to cool completely.

TOP: *Nutty Crescents*
BOTTOM: *Irish Lace Cookies*

COFFEE CREAM CRUMBLES

These cookies can be made ahead and stored, but only sandwich them together on the day of eating.

◆ ◆ ◆

1 CUP UNSALTED BUTTER

²/₃ CUP CONFECTIONERS' SUGAR

4 TEASPOONS INSTANT COFFEE DISSOLVED IN

1 TABLESPOON HOT WATER

3 CUPS ALL-PURPOSE FLOUR

FILLING

1 CUP CONFECTIONERS' SUGAR

¹/₄ CUP UNSALTED BUTTER

2 TABLESPOONS LIGHT CREAM

CONFECTIONERS' SUGAR TO DUST

M A K E S   A B O U T   2 0

◆ ◆ ◆

Put the butter and confectioners' sugar into a bowl and beat together until light and creamy. Add the dissolved coffee to the mixture. Sift in the flour and work together to make a soft dough.

Place the dough in a piping bag fitted with a star tip and pipe out stars onto greased baking sheets. Bake at 350°F for 10-12 minutes. Transfer to a wire rack to cool.

To make the buttercream filling, beat together the ingredients until creamy (but do not overbeat). Place the buttercream in a small piping bag fitted with a small star tip and pipe a swirl on half of the cookies. Sandwich with the remaining cookies and dust the tops with confectioners' sugar.

APRICOT ALMANDINES

Use a good-quality apricot conserve for these cookies. Do not keep them any longer than 2 days as they will soften.

◆ ◆ ◆

2 CUPS ALL-PURPOSE FLOUR

¹/₂ CUP CONFECTIONERS' SUGAR

³/₄ CUP UNSALTED BUTTER

1 CUP GROUND ALMONDS

1 TEASPOON ALMOND EXTRACT

1 EGG, SEPARATED

¹/₂ CUP CHOPPED BLANCHED ALMONDS

4 TABLESPOONS APRICOT CONSERVE

M A K E S   2 8

◆ ◆ ◆

Sift the flour and confectioners' sugar into a bowl, add the butter and rub in to make a fine textured mixture. Stir in the ground almonds, then mix to a dough with the almond extract and egg yolk. Knead until smooth, then wrap and chill for 30 minutes.

Roll out the dough thinly to about ¹/₈th inch then cut out small rounds with a 2-inch fancy cutter. Cut out the centers from half and place on greased baking sheets. Brush the rings with egg white, and sprinkle with the chopped almonds. Bake at 375°F for 10-12 minutes until golden. Transfer to a wire rack to cool.

Spread the rounds with conserve and cover with the almond-covered rings.

TOP: *Coffee Cream Crumbles*
BOTTOM: *Apricot Almandines*

MOCHA SLICES

◆ ◆ ◆

$^2/_3$ CUP BUTTER

5 TABLESPOONS SIFTED RAW SUGAR

1 EGG, BEATEN

$1^1/_2$ CUPS SELF-RISING FLOUR

1 TABLESPOON UNSWEETENED COCOA

MOCHA CREAM

$^1/_4$ CUP UNSALTED BUTTER

$^3/_4$ CUP CONFECTIONERS' SUGAR

2 TEASPOONS INSTANT COFFEE DISSOLVED IN

1 TEASPOON HOT WATER

2 SQUARES DARK CHOCOLATE, MELTED

ICING

1 CUP SIFTED CONFECTIONERS' SUGAR

2 TEASPOONS INSTANT COFFEE DISSOLVED IN

4 TEASPOONS HOT WATER

$1^1/_2$ SQUARES DARK CHOCOLATE, MELTED

MAKES 14 SLICES

◆ ◆ ◆

Cream the butter and raw sugar until fluffy, add the egg and beat again. Sift in the flour and cocoa, and beat until smooth. Press evenly into a lined 9 x 13-inch jelly roll tin. Bake at 350°F for 12-15 minutes. Invert onto a wire rack and peel away the paper. Cut the pastry in half across the middle.

Put all the ingredients for the mocha cream into a bowl and beat together until smooth. Spread over one half of the pastry, then sandwich the other on top.

Add the dissolved coffee to the confectioners' sugar and mix until smooth. Spread over the top of the pastry. Quickly pipe lines of chocolate across the glaze, then draw a skewer through to give a feather effect. Allow to set before cutting into fingers.

PECAN AND MAPLE HEARTS

A delicious combination of flavors, these cookies would make a special gift for friends or family.

◆ ◆ ◆

$^3/_4$ CUP UNSALTED BUTTER

$^1/_2$ CUP SIFTED RAW SUGAR

$2^1/_4$ CUPS ALL-PURPOSE FLOUR

$^3/_4$ CUP FINELY CHOPPED PECANS

FILLING

1 CUP CONFECTIONERS' SUGAR

$^1/_4$ CUP BUTTER

3 TABLESPOONS MAPLE SYRUP

CONFECTIONERS' SUGAR TO DUST

MAKES 20

◆ ◆ ◆

Put the butter and sugar into a bowl and beat together until creamy. Stir in the flour and nuts, and work together to make a smooth dough. Knead lightly, then wrap in plastic wrap and chill for 30 minutes.

Roll out thinly, and using a medium-sized heart-shaped cutter, cut out the cookies. Place on greased baking sheets and bake at 375°F for 8-10 minutes. Transfer to a wire rack to cool.

To make the filling, beat the confectioners' sugar and butter together. Beat in the maple syrup, then spread over half of the cookies. Sandwich with the remaining cookies and dust with confectioners' sugar.

TOP: *Pecan and Maple Hearts*
BOTTOM: *Mocha Slices*

PAN BAKES

The cookies in this chapter are all baked in a large block, cooled, then cut into squares, bars, fingers, triangles or diamonds. They are easy to make as they do not require special shaping. Often moist and chewy, they are an excellent standby for hungry children and with the addition of high-fiber ingredients they make healthy snacks for lunch-boxes or picnics.

A variety of shallow baking pans have been used in these recipes. Most kitchens have a jelly roll pan, but do try to use a pan with the measurements specified in each recipe, as the quantity of ingredients has been calculated for the size recommended.

In some recipes it is suggested that the pan is lined; this will help ease out the cookies after baking. Pan-baked cookies are cooled in the pan before being cut into shapes.

Most cookies can be frozen successfully either in their raw state or after baking; it is better to freeze baked cookies undecorated. Open-freeze cookies until solid, then pack in rigid containers for storage. Cover and label the container and store for up to two months. Freezing cookies means you can always offer homemade treats when unexpected guests arrive. Thaw baked cookies for about 15 minutes at room temperature. Unbaked piped, shaped or pan-baked cookies can be baked without thawing; simply follow the recipe and add a few minutes to the baking time.

CONTENTS

◆ ◆ ◆

STRAWBERRY LINZER BARS

Adapted from the Viennese dessert, Linzertorte, these cookies can be made with your favorite conserve. Use a good-quality conserve with a high proportion of fruit.

◆ ◆ ◆

3/4 CUP BUTTER

1 CUP SUPERFINE SUGAR

1 EGG, BEATEN

GRATED RIND OF 1 LEMON

2 CUPS ALL-PURPOSE FLOUR

1 TEASPOON GROUND CINNAMON

1 CUP GROUND ALMONDS

3/4 CUP STRAWBERRY CONSERVE

CONFECTIONERS' SUGAR TO DUST

MAKES 24

◆ ◆ ◆

In a bowl beat the butter and sugar together until light and creamy. Beat in the egg and lemon rind. Sift the flour and cinnamon together, then add to the mixture with the ground almonds to make a dough.

Turn onto a floured surface and knead lightly, wrap in plastic wrap and refrigerate for 30 minutes.

Take two-thirds of the dough and press into a greased 9 x 13-inch jelly roll pan. Spread over the conserve.

With floured hands, roll small pieces of the remaining dough into pencil-thin strips. Arrange the strips over the conserve in a lattice pattern. Chill for 30 minutes.

Bake at 350°F for about 35-40 minutes until golden and cooked through. Allow to cool in the pan. Dust with confectioners' sugar, then cut into bars.

DATE BUTTER COOKIES

Do not use ready-chopped, sugar-coated dates or any with a sticky coating for this recipe or it will be too sweet.

◆ ◆ ◆

3/4 CUP BUTTER

1/3 CUP GOLDEN SUPERFINE SUGAR

1 1/2 CUPS SELF-RISING FLOUR

1/2 CUP GROUND RICE

1 1/4 CUPS CHOPPED PITTED DATES

MAKES 16

◆ ◆ ◆

Cream the butter and sugar together until light and fluffy. Stir in the rest of the ingredients and mix well.

Turn the mixture into a greased shallow pan 7 x 11 inches. Level the surface and prick all over with a fork.

Bake at 350°F for 10 minutes. Mark into fingers, then return to the oven and cook for a further 10 minutes until golden.

Allow to cool in the pan. With a sharp knife cut through again into fingers and remove from the pan.

LEFT: *Date Butter Cookies*
RIGHT: *Strawberry Linzer Bars*

POPPYSEED APRICOT COOKIES

The apricots add a delicious tang to these cookies. Ready-to-eat fruit needs no soaking.

◆ ◆ ◆

$^3/_4$ CUP READY-TO-EAT DRIED APRICOTS

$^1/_2$ CUP GOLDEN GRANULATED SUGAR

$^3/_4$ CUP BUTTER OR MARGARINE

1 LARGE EGG, BEATEN

1 TABLESPOON LEMON JUICE

3 CUPS SELF-RISING FLOUR

2 TABLESPOONS POPPYSEEDS

$^2/_3$ CUP CONFECTIONERS' SUGAR

MAKES ABOUT 24

◆ ◆ ◆

Place the apricots in a pan with 2 tablespoons of the granulated sugar and 4 tablespoons water. Simmer for 5 minutes. Cool slightly, then work to a rough textured purée in a blender or food processor.

Put the butter or margarine into a bowl with the remaining granulated sugar and beat until light and fluffy. Add the egg and lemon juice, then add the flour and poppyseeds and mix to a softish dough.

Divide the dough into three pieces. Roll each to a rope about 10 inches long, then pat out to make a rectangle 2 inches wide. Press down the middle to make a channel, spread the apricot purée down the middle of each. Transfer to greased baking sheets and bake at 350°F for 18-20 minutes.

Mix the confectioners' sugar with a little water to make a thin glaze, then drizzle from a spoon over the cooled cookies and allow to set. Cut the logs into slices.

CHOCOLATE PECAN BARS

A wonderful combination of chocolate and nuts; these will not last long enough to be stored in the cookie jar.

◆ ◆ ◆

$^1/_2$ CUP BUTTER

$1^1/_2$ CUPS ALL-PURPOSE FLOUR

TOPPING

$^1/_4$ CUP BUTTER

4 SQUARES DARK CHOCOLATE

$^1/_3$ CUP LIGHT CORN SYRUP

$^2/_3$ CUP RAW SUGAR

$^1/_2$ TEASPOON VANILLA EXTRACT

3 EGGS, BEATEN

$1^1/_2$ CUPS ROUGHLY CHOPPED PECAN NUTS

MAKES 24

◆ ◆ ◆

Rub the butter into the flour and bind together with cold water to make a pastry dough. Use to line a jelly roll pan 8 x 12 inches. Trim the edges.

Melt the butter and chocolate in a bowl over a pan of simmering water. Put the syrup, sugar, vanilla extract and eggs into a large bowl and whisk until light and frothy, then whisk in the melted mixture. Pour over the dough and scatter over the nuts.

Bake at 350°F for about 50 minutes until the filling feels firm. Allow to cool in the pan then cut into bars $1^1/_2$ x 3 inches.

TOP: *Poppyseed Apricot Cookies*
BOTTOM: *Chocolate Pecan Bars*

FIGGY ROLLS

These cookies with a hint of orange are really tasty.

◆ ◆ ◆

2 CUPS SELF-RISING FLOUR

1 TEASPOON APPLE PIE SPICE

5 TABLESPOONS SIFTED RAW SUGAR

$^1/_2$ CUP UNSALTED BUTTER

1 EGG. BEATEN

FILLING

$1^1/_2$ CUPS READY-TO-EAT DRIED FIGS

5 TABLESPOONS RAW SUGAR

GRATED RIND AND JUICE OF 1 LARGE ORANGE

$^1/_3$ CUP CRUSHED DRY SPONGE FINGERS

TOPPING

MILK

GOLDEN GRANUALTED SUGAR

MAKES 30

◆ ◆ ◆

Sift the flour and spice into a bowl. Rub in the butter, then add the sugar and egg. Mix to a dough, then knead until smooth. Wrap and refrigerate.

Place the figs in a saucepan with $^2/_3$ cup water and simmer for 10 minutes. Add the sugar and orange rind and juice, and simmer until most of the liquid has evaporated. Purée, then allow to cool. Stir in the crumbs.

Divide the dough into 2 and roll out each piece to 6 x 12 inches. Place half the fig mixture down the center of each strip, dampen the edges with a little milk, then roll up. Place on a greased baking sheet with the joins underneath. Brush with milk and sprinkle with sugar. Bake at 375°F for 20 minutes. When cold cut each roll into 15 slices.

MARMALADE CRUNCHIES

Another wholesome treat to keep in the cookie jar.

◆ ◆ ◆

$2^1/_4$ CUPS CRUNCHY OAT CEREAL

$^1/_2$ CUP CHOPPED MIXED NUTS

1 CUP WHOLEWHEAT SELF-RISING FLOUR

$^3/_4$ CUP MARGARINE

2 TABLESPOONS LIGHT CORN SYRUP

5 TABLESPOONS COARSE-CUT SEVILLE

ORANGE MARMALADE

MAKES 16

◆ ◆ ◆

Put the crunchy oat cereal into a plastic bag and crush with a rolling pin. Tip into a bowl and mix with the nuts and flour.

Melt the margarine with the golden syrup, then pour onto the dry ingredients and mix together. Press half of the mixture into the base of a greased 8-inch shallow square pan. Spread over the marmalade, then top with the remaining oat mixture, pressing down gently.

Bake at 350°F for 25 minutes. Cool slightly, then mark into small squares. Leave in the pan to cool. Use a sharp knife to cut up the squares.

TOP: *Figgy Rolls*
BOTTOM: *Marmalade Crunchies*

CHOCOLATE CARAMELS

A very sweet cookie, but a very popular one too!

◆ ◆ ◆

$^1/_2$ CUP BUTTER

$1^1/_2$ CUPS ALL-PURPOSE FLOUR

$^1/_4$ CUP GOLDEN SUPERFINE SUGAR

FILLING

$^3/_4$ CUP BUTTER

$^1/_2$ CUP GOLDEN SUPERFINE SUGAR

3 TABLESPOONS LIGHT CORN SYRUP

1 x 14 OZ CAN CONDENSED SKIMMED MILK

TOPPING

6 SQUARES DARK CHOCOLATE

2 TABLESPOONS UNSALTED BUTTER

MAKES 24

◆ ◆ ◆

Line a 9-inch shallow square pan with non-stick baking parchment paper. Rub the butter into the flour, stir in the sugar, then turn into the prepared pan and press down. Bake at 350°F for 20-25 minutes until golden.

Meanwhile, put the filling ingredients into a saucepan and melt over a low heat. When all the sugar has dissolved, bring to a boil and simmer for 6-8 minutes, stirring all the time until it becomes very thick. Pour over the base and refrigerate until firm.

Melt the chocolate and butter together, mix until smooth and allow to cool. Spread over the caramel, then chill again until set. With a sharp knife, cut into pieces about $1^1/_2$ x 2 inches.

ENGLISH FLAPJACKS

Very quick and easy to make, these cookies are an ideal treat for children's lunch boxes or after-school snack.

◆ ◆ ◆

$2^1/_4$ CUPS ROLLED OATS

1 CUP LIGHTLY TOASTED HAZELNUTS, CHOPPED

$^1/_2$ CUP WHOLEWHEAT FLOUR

$^1/_2$ CUP BUTTER OR MARGARINE

2 TABLESPOONS CLEAR HONEY

$^1/_2$ CUP RAW SUGAR

MAKES 12 OR 24 PIECES

◆ ◆ ◆

Put the oats, hazelnuts and flour into a large bowl and mix together. In a saucepan heat the butter or margarine with the honey and sugar until melted. Pour onto the dry ingredients and mix well.

Turn into a greased 9-inch square shallow pan and level, pressing down with the back of a spoon.

Bake at 350°F for 20-25 minutes until golden and firm to the touch. Mark into 12 or 24 pieces and allow to cool in the pan. Cut through with a sharp knife and remove.

TOP: *Chocolate Caramels*
BOTTOM: *English Flapjacks*

TUTTI FRUTTI SQUARES

*Packed with delicious fruit, these cookies
will appeal to all ages — perfect for packed
lunches and picnics.*

◆ ◆ ◆

1 CUP WHOLEWHEAT SELF-RISING FLOUR

$^2/_3$ CUP RAW SUGAR

$^1/_4$ CUP BUTTER OR MARGARINE

TOPPING

$^2/_3$ CUP GOLDEN RAISINS

$^2/_3$ CUP SHREDDED COCONUT

$^2/_3$ CUP CHOPPED CANDIED CHERRIES

$^1/_3$ CUP MIXED CANDIED PEEL

2 EGGS, BEATEN

5 TABLESPOONS RAW SUGAR

$^1/_2$ CUP WHOLEWHEAT SELF-RISING FLOUR

MAKES 15

◆ ◆ ◆

Sift the flour and sugar together into a bowl. Add the
butter or margarine and rub in to resemble fine
crumbs.

Turn into a greased 7 x 11-inch shallow baking pan
and press down evenly. Bake at 325°F for 10-12 minutes until light golden. Remove from the oven.

Meanwhile, put all the topping ingredients into a bowl
and mix together. Spread evenly over the shortbread
base and return to the oven to bake for 30 minutes.

Cool slightly before marking into squares. Leave in the
pan until cold before cutting up.

DUTCH CINNAMON COOKIES

*The Dutch are very fond of their cookies
and morning coffee and afternoon tea
are always accompanied by something from
the local bakery. Some Dutch towns
have been famous for hundreds of years for
their particular specialties made with
butter and spices.*

◆ ◆ ◆

2 CUPS ALL-PURPOSE FLOUR

$1^1/_2$ TEASPOONS GROUND CINNAMON

$^1/_2$ CUP UNSALTED BUTTER

$^1/_3$ CUP GOLDEN SUPERFINE SUGAR

MAKES 16

◆ ◆ ◆

Sift the flour and cinnamon into a bowl, rub in the butter until the mixture resembles fine crumbs. Stir in the
sugar, then turn into a lightly greased 7 x 11-inch shallow baking pan. Press the mixture evenly into the pan
then rough up the surface with a fork. Chill for 1 hour.

Bake at 350°F for 20-25 minutes until golden. While
still hot use a sharp knife and cut into 16 bars.

TOP: *Tutti Frutti Squares*
BOTTOM: *Dutch Cinnamon Cookies*

CHERRY ALMOND BAKEWELLS

A great recipe for a special occasion.

❖ ❖ ❖

1/2 CUP BUTTER OR MARGARINE

1 1/2 CUPS ALL-PURPOSE FLOUR

2 TABLESPOONS SUPERFINE SUGAR

4-5 TABLESPOONS CHERRY CONSERVE

TOPPING

1/2 CUP SOFT MARGARINE

1/2 CUP GOLDEN SUPERFINE SUGAR

2 EGGS

3/4 CUP SELF-RISING FLOUR

3/4 CUP GROUND ALMONDS

1/2 TEASPOON ALMOND EXTRACT

1/2 CUP SLIVERED ALMONDS

ICING

1 TABLESPOON UNSALTED BUTTER

3/4 CUP CONFECTIONERS' SUGAR

1-2 TABLESPOONS LEMON JUICE

MAKES 24

❖ ❖ ❖

Rub the butter or margarine into the flour, add the sugar, then mix with a little cold water to make a pastry dough. Knead lightly, then roll out and line a jelly roll pan 8 x 12 inches. Spread over the conserve.

Put the topping ingredients into a bowl and beat for 2 minutes, then spoon onto the conserve and level the surface. Scatter over the slivered almonds then bake at 350°F for 25-30 minutes until golden.

Beat the remaining butter and confectioners' sugar with enough lemon juice to make a thick frosting. Place in a small parchment paper bag and drizzle over the cooled pan bake. Allow to set, then cut into bars.

NUTTY HONEY DIAMONDS

For anyone who likes nuts,
this will be a winner.

❖ ❖ ❖

1/2 CUP MARGARINE

1/3 CUP GOLDEN SUPERFINE SUGAR

1 EGG, BEATEN

1 1/2 CUPS WHOLEWHEAT SELF-RISING FLOUR

TOPPING

1 CUP FINELY CHOPPED WALNUTS

1 CUP CHOPPED WHOLE ALMONDS

6 TABLESPOONS CLEAR HONEY

2 EGGS, BEATEN

WALNUT HALVES TO DECORATE

MAKES 16

❖ ❖ ❖

Cream the margarine and sugar together until light and fluffy. Add the egg, then the flour and mix to make a dough. Press into the base of a greased oblong shallow pan, 8 1/2 x 11 1/2 inches and bake at 350°F for 10-12 minutes until golden.

To make the topping, combine the nuts with half of the honey and the eggs. Spoon over the base and return to the oven for 15-20 minutes until richly golden.

Brush the remaining honey over the top. Cut into diamonds (there will be some small triangles left in the corners) and decorate each with a walnut half. Cool in the pan before removing.

TOP: *Nutty Honey Diamonds*
BOTTOM: *Cherry Almond Bakewells*

COCONUT SQUARES

Take care not to overcook these delicious cookies, otherwise the coconut topping will harden and lose its moist texture.

◆ ◆ ◆

$1/_2$ CUP BUTTER OR MARGARINE

$1/_3$ CUP GOLDEN SUPERFINE SUGAR

2 EGG YOLKS

$1^1/_2$ CUPS SELF-RISING FLOUR

$2/_3$ CUP SHREDDED COCONUT

6 TABLESPOONS WARMED RASPBERRY CONSERVE

TOPPING

3 EGG WHITES

1 CUP CONFECTIONERS' SUGAR

$1^3/_4$ CUPS SHREDDED COCONUT

MAKES 28

◆ ◆ ◆

Beat the butter or margarine with the sugar until creamy, add the egg yolks and beat again. Stir in the flour and coconut and mix together. Press into the base of a greased oblong shallow pan $8^1/_2$ x $11^1/_2$ inches. Bake at 350°F for 10 minutes.

Spread the conserve over the base. Whisk the egg whites until stiff, fold in the confectioners' sugar and coconut, then spoon over the conserve. Gently level out with a fork and return to the oven at 300°F for 30-40 minutes until light golden. Cool in the pan, then cut into squares.

SESAME TRIANGLES

A thin cookie packed with lots of flavor and goodness.

◆ ◆ ◆

$1^1/_4$ CUPS MEDIUM OATMEAL

$1/_2$ CUP LIGHTLY ROASTED SESAME SEEDS

5 TABLESPOONS SIFTED RAW SUGAR

4 TABLESPOONS CLEAR HONEY

5 TABLESPOONS SUNFLOWER OIL

MAKES 24

◆ ◆ ◆

Put the dry ingredients into a bowl and mix together. Add the honey and oil, and mix again.

Line a 8 x 12-inch jelly roll pan with non-stick baking parchment paper, then turn the mixture into the pan. Level with a palette knife and bake at 350°F for 20-25 minutes.

Cool for 2 minutes, then cut into 12 squares and across into triangles. Allow to cool completely before removing from the paper.

TOP: *Coconut Squares*
BOTTOM: *Sesame Triangles*

APPLE CINNAMON CRUMBLES

These are best eaten the same day, because the apple filling will make them soft if kept.

◆ ◆ ◆

1 CUP SELF-RISING FLOUR

1 CUP ALL-PURPOSE FLOUR

1 TABLESPOON GROUND CINNAMON

$^1/_2$ CUP CONFECTIONERS' SUGAR

$^3/_4$ CUP GROUND ALMONDS

$^3/_4$ CUP BUTTER

1 EGG, BEATEN

1 POUND COOKING APPLES

3 TABLESPOONS GOLDEN GRANULATED SUGAR

M A K E S   3 2

◆ ◆ ◆

Sift the flours with 2 teaspoons of cinnamon and the confectioners' sugar. Add the ground almonds, then rub in the butter. Mix to a dough with the egg, turn onto a floured surface and knead until smooth.

Take one-third of the dough, wrap and freeze it until hard. Press the remaining dough into a greased jelly roll pan 8 x 12 inches and refrigerate.

Bake the dough in the pan for 10 minutes at 350°F. Grate the apples with the skin on. Mix with 2 tablespoons of the granulated sugar and spread over the base. Coarsely grate the frozen dough and scatter over the apple. Mix the remaining cinnamon and sugar together, sprinkle on top, then bake for a further 25 minutes. Cut into 32 pieces when cold.

GLAZED LEMON SHORTIES

A delicious variation on shortbread.

◆ ◆ ◆

$^3/_4$ CUP SOFTENED UNSALTED BUTTER

$^1/_4$ CUP SUPERFINE SUGAR

1 TABLESPOON GRATED LEMON RIND

1 TABLESPOON LEMON JUICE

2 CUPS ALL-PURPOSE FLOUR

$^1/_2$ CUP GROUND RICE

GLAZE

5 TABLESPOONS CONFECTIONERS' SUGAR

1 TABLESPOON LEMON JUICE

M A K E S   2 4

◆ ◆ ◆

Cream the butter and sugar together until light and fluffy, add the lemon rind and juice and beat again.

Fold in the flour and ground rice, and mix well to form a firm dough. Knead lightly until smooth, then cut the dough in half.

Roll out each piece to a rectangle 3 x 12 inches and place on greased baking sheets. Chill for 30 minutes.

Bake at 350°F for 25-30 minutes until golden. Mix the confectioners' sugar with the lemon juice and brush over the shortbread. With a sharp knife cut into wedges and transfer to a wire rack to cool.

TOP: *Glazed Lemon Shorties*
BOTTOM: *Apple Cinnamon Crumbles*

FESTIVE COOKIES

Throughout the seasons and in every country certain cookies are traditionally baked for special occasions. They are often associated with religious festivals, for example, or the recipe may be based simply on an ingredient plentiful in that part of the world. They are all variations on a basic mixture; it is the shape or decoration which gives them their special significance.

Although many cookies can be stored for two or three weeks in airtight containers, they do tend to dry out and lose the delicious flavor of freshly baked cookies. For ideal storing, line the bottom of the container with waxed paper and place another sheet of paper between each two layers of cookies or between each single layer of soft ones. Store different types of cookies in separate containers. Cookies filled with jelly or buttercream should be eaten soon after filling. If you want to make them ahead of time, you can bake cookies and fill or decorate them shortly before serving. Should plain cookies lose their crispness during storage, return them to the oven at 325°F for about 5 minutes.

If you are making cookies to give away, encourage the recipient to eat them as soon as possible while they are still fresh. Cookies that are hung on Christmas trees should not be left too long before eating as they will become stale; allow the children to eat them daily and replace them from the cookie tin.

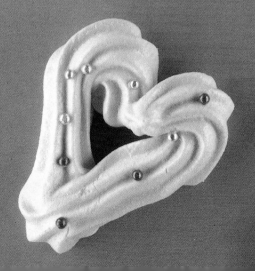

CONTENTS

◆ ◆ ◆

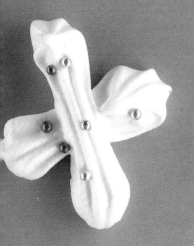

VALENTINE KNOTS

A lovely combination of chocolate and walnut flavors to make very pretty shaped cookies.

◆ ◆ ◆

3/4 CUP BUTTER

1/2 CUP SUPERFINE SUGAR

2 TABLESPOONS BRANDY

FEW DROPS OF VANILLA EXTRACT

2 1/4 CUPS ALL-PURPOSE FLOUR

1 SQUARE FINELY GRATED DARK CHOCOLATE

1/4 CUP FINELY CHOPPED WALNUTS

M A K E S   2 7

◆ ◆ ◆

Put the butter and sugar into a bowl and beat until light and fluffy, add the brandy and vanilla extract. Sift in the flour, then mix until the crumbly stage is reached. Divide the mixture into two, add the chocolate to one and the walnuts to the other. Work each together to make a smooth dough, then wrap and chill for 30 minutes.

Divide each piece of dough into 27 small balls. Take one of each flavor and roll out into a thin ropes about 5 inches long using your fingers, then twist them together, form into a circle and pinch the ends together. Place on a greased baking sheet. Repeat with the remaining dough. Bake at 350°F for 12-15 minutes. Transfer to a wire rack to cool.

MERINGUE HEARTS AND KISSES

A fun way of making meringues. Color some of the mixture with pink food coloring if wished.

◆ ◆ ◆

3 EGG WHITES

3/4 CUP SUPERFINE SUGAR

COLORED SUGAR BALLS TO DECORATE

M A K E S   A B O U T   2 0

◆ ◆ ◆

Put the egg whites into a clean bowl and whisk until stiff and dry. Gradually whisk in half the sugar, keeping the mixture stiff and glossy. Carefully fold in the remaining sugar. Place the meringue in a piping bag fitted with a 1/2-inch star tip and pipe hearts and kisses onto baking sheets lined with non-stick baking parchment paper. Scatter over colored sugar balls.

Bake at 250°F for about 1 hour or until crisp. When cool, peel off the lining paper.

TOP: *Valentine Knots*

BOTTOM: *Meringue Hearts and Kisses*

POPPYSEED POUCHES

These pastries, Hamentaschen, are traditional for the Jewish festival of Purim.

◆ ◆ ◆

$^2/_3$ CUP BUTTER OR MARGARINE

$^1/_2$ CUP SUPERFINE SUGAR

1 EGG, BEATEN

FEW DROPS OF VANILLA EXTRACT

$2^1/_2$ CUPS ALL-PURPOSE FLOUR

1 TEASPOON BAKING POWDER

$^1/_2$ CUP SUPERFINE SUGAR

$^3/_4$ CUP POPPYSEEDS

1 TABLESPOON CLEAR HONEY

GRATED RIND AND JUICE OF $^1/_2$ LEMON

$^1/_2$ TEASPOON GROUND CINNAMON

$^1/_3$ CUP CHOPPED RAISINS

$^1/_4$ CUP FINELY CHOPPED ALMONDS

1 SMALL EGG, BEATEN

MAKES 30-36

◆ ◆ ◆

Beat the butter and sugar until fluffy, beat in the egg and extract. Sift in the flour and baking powder and mix to form a dough. Knead lightly, then wrap and chill.

Heat the sugar with 4 tablespoons water until dissolved, then bring to boil. Add the poppy seeds, honey, lemon rind and juice and cinnamon. Bring back to a boil, stirring. Add the raisins, nuts and egg. Cool.

Roll out the dough to $^1/_8$th inch and cut out 3-inch rounds with a fluted cutter. Put a teaspoon of filling in the center of each, brush edges with water, then bring them to the center to form a tricorn. Place on greased baking sheets and chill for 30 minutes. Bake at 350°F for 15-20 minutes.

CREAM CHEESE COOKIES

These cinnamon and walnut filled cookies are also known as Rugelach. The pastry is made with cream cheese and is popular in Israel.

◆ ◆ ◆

$^1/_2$ CUP BUTTER

$^1/_2$ CUP CREAM CHEESE

2 TEASPOONS LEMON JUICE

2 CUPS ALL-PURPOSE FLOUR

2 EGG YOLKS

FILLING

5 TABLESPOONS RAW SUGAR

1 TEASPOON GROUND CINNAMON

$^1/_2$ CUP CHOPPED RAISINS

1 CUP FINELY CHOPPED WALNUTS

TO DECORATE

GRANULATED SUGAR

MAKES 28

◆ ◆ ◆

Put the butter and cream cheese into a bowl and beat together until creamy. Add the lemon juice and then the flour and egg yolks, and mix to form a smooth dough. Knead lightly, wrap, and chill for 30 minutes.

Mix ingredients for the filling together and set aside.

Divide the dough in half, roll one half out to a circle 10 inches in diameter. Using a crimped pastry wheel, cut the round into 14 wedges. Spread half the filling over the wedges, then roll up from the wide end. Place on a greased baking sheet. Repeat the procedure with the remaining dough and filling. Sprinkle with sugar and bake at 350°F for 20 minutes until golden.

EASTER CURRANT COOKIES

The rum glaze on these cookies makes them very special. Substitute orange juice if making them for children.

◆ ◆ ◆

3/4 CUP BUTTER OR MARGARINE

3/4 CUP SUPERFINE SUGAR

1 EGG, BEATEN

2 TABLESPOONS RUM

1/3 CUP CHOPPED MIXED PEEL

3/4 CUP CURRANTS

3 CUPS ALL-PURPOSE FLOUR

1 TEASPOON APPLE PIE SPICE

GLAZE

2/3 CUP CONFECTIONERS' SUGAR

1 TABLESPOON DARK RUM

2 TABLESPOONS WARMED APRICOT CONSERVE

MAKES ABOUT 24

◆ ◆ ◆

Put the butter or margarine into a bowl with the sugar and beat together until light and fluffy. Beat in the egg and rum. Stir in the mixed peel and currants, then sift in the flour and spices. Mix together to make a firm dough. Knead lightly until smooth.

Roll out the dough to 1/4 inch thick and use a 2-inch cutter to stamp out the cookies. Place them on greased baking sheets and bake at 350°F for 10-15 minutes.

Meanwhile, sift the confectioners' sugar into a bowl, add the rum and mix to make a runny glaze.

Remove the cookies from the oven, and while still hot, brush with the apricot conserve and then with the glaze. Transfer to a wire rack to cool.

FESTIVE ORANGE COOKIES

This is both an attractive and delicious cookie which is worth making for a festive celebration, or to give as a gift.

◆ ◆ ◆

1/2 CUP UNSALTED BUTTER, SOFTENED

5 TABLESPOONS CONFECTIONERS' SUGAR

GRATED RIND OF 1 LARGE ORANGE

2 TABLESPOONS ORANGE JUICE

1 1/2 CUPS ALL-PURPOSE FLOUR

TO DECORATE

2 SQUARES DARK CHOCOLATE

2 SQUARES WHITE CHOCOLATE

MAKES 15

◆ ◆ ◆

Beat the butter and confectioners' sugar together until light and creamy, then beat in the orange rind and juice. Sift in the flour and mix to make a soft dough. Spoon the mixture into a piping bag fitted with a large star tip and pipe circles about 3 inches in diameter onto greased baking sheets. Chill for about 45 minutes.

Bake the cookies at 325°F for 10-12 minutes. Transfer to a wire rack to cool completely.

Melt the chocolates separately in bowls placed over simmering water. Place each in a small parchment paper piping bag and pipe drizzles over each cookie. Leave to set.

TOP: *Festive Orange Cookies*
BOTTOM: *Easter Currant Cookies*

HIGHLAND SHORTBREAD

This recipe can be made into different shapes of shortbread. If a mold is available, use to make a traditional shortbread in the Scottish style. Alternatively, cut into small rounds and decorate.

◆ ◆ ◆

1 CUP BUTTER

$1/2$ CUP SUPERFINE SUGAR

2 CUPS ALL-PURPOSE FLOUR

1 CUP GROUND RICE OR CORNSTARCH

$1/2$ TEASPOON GRATED NUTMEG

SUPERFINE SUGAR TO DUST

MAKES 2 LARGE SHORTBREAD AND 16-20 SMALL ONES

◆ ◆ ◆

Put the butter and sugar into a bowl and beat until light and creamy. Sift in the flour, ground rice or cornstarch and nutmeg and work by hand to make a soft dough. Knead the dough on a lightly floured surface.

Take one-third of the dough and roll out to a round approximately 7 inches in diameter. Prick with a fork and pinch the edges. Place on a greased baking sheet. Mark into 8 pieces. Refrigerate for 1 hour.

Roll out the remaining dough about $1/8$th inch thick and cut into rounds using a 3-inch cutter. Place on greased baking sheets and prick the surfaces with a fork. Bake in the oven at 350°F for about 15 minutes – the large round will take 20-25 minutes – until pale golden. Sprinkle with superfine sugar. Cool on the baking sheets for 15 minutes, then transfer to a wire rack to cool completely.

CHRISTMAS FRUIT AND NUT COOKIES

Let the children help make these cookies during their vacation, they will make a welcome change to mincemeat tartlets!

◆ ◆ ◆

$1/2$ CUP SOFT MARGARINE

$2/3$ CUP SIFTED RAW SUGAR

1 EGG, BEATEN

2 CUPS SELF-RISING FLOUR

1 TEASPOON APPLE PIE SPICE

$1/2$ CUP CHOPPED READY-TO-EAT APRICOTS

$2/3$ CUP CHOPPED CANDIED CHERRIES

$3/4$ CUP SLIVERED BLANCHED ALMONDS

BEATEN EGG TO GLAZE

GRANULATED SUGAR TO DUST

MAKES 22-24

◆ ◆ ◆

Put the margarine and sugar into a bowl and beat together until creamy. Add the egg and beat again. Sift in the flour and spice, then add the apricots, cherries and $1/2$ cup of the almonds. Mix all the ingredients together.

Drop dessert spoonfuls of the mixture onto greased baking sheets and flatten the surface with a fork. Brush the tops of the cookies with beaten egg to glaze, then scatter over the remaining almonds.

Bake at 350°F for 15-20 minutes until golden. Transfer to a wire rack to cool. If wished, the tops can be sprinkled with a little granulated sugar.

TOP: *Highland Shortbread*
BOTTOM: *Christmas Fruit and Nut Cookies*

LEBKUCHEN

Spicy German Lebkuchen are traditionally eaten on St Nicholas Day, December 6th.

◆ ◆ ◆

3 EGGS

1 CUP LESS 2 TABLESPOONS SUGAR

1 3/4 CUPS GROUND ALMONDS

1/3 CUP FINELY CHOPPED CANDIED PEEL

1/2 CUP ALL-PURPOSE FLOUR

1 TEASPOON GROUND CINNAMON

1/2 TEASPOON GROUND CARDAMON

GOOD PINCH OF GINGER, ALLSPICE AND

GROUND CLOVES

TO DECORATE

4 SQUARES DARK CHOCOLATE, MELTED

2/3 CUP CONFECTIONERS' SUGAR

SUGAR STRANDS OR SPRINKLES

M A K E S   A B O U T   6 0

◆ ◆ ◆

Put the eggs and sugar into a bowl, stand over a pan of simmering water and whisk until thick and foamy. Remove the bowl from the pan and continue to whisk for 2 minutes (or longer for thicker cookies).

Combine the remaining ingredients together, then stir into the egg mixture. Drop heaped teaspoonfuls onto baking sheets lined with non-stick baking parchment paper, spreading them gently into smooth mounds. Bake at 325°F for 15-20 minutes, until light brown and slightly soft to the touch. Slide the cookies onto wire racks to cool. Peel off the paper when cold.

Mix confectioners' sugar with a little water to make a thin glaze, dip half of the cookies in this and the rest in the melted chocolate. Sprinkle with sugar decorations.

CANE COOKIES

These are fun cookies for children – super for parties. Tie ribbons around them and hang them on the Christmas tree.

◆ ◆ ◆

3/4 CUP SOFT MARGARINE

1/2 CUP CONFECTIONERS' SUGAR

1 TEASPOON GRATED LEMON RIND

1/4 CUP CORNSTARCH

1 3/4 CUPS ALL-PURPOSE FLOUR

1 TABLESPOON MILK

TO DECORATE

1 CUP CONFECTIONERS' SUGAR

SUGAR STRANDS OR NONPAREIL

M A K E S   A B O U T   2 0

◆ ◆ ◆

Put the margarine and sugar into a bowl and beat until soft and creamy. Add the lemon rind. Sift in the cornstarch and flour and mix to a soft dough, using the milk if necessary.

Place the mixture in a piping bag fitted with a star tip and pipe walking cane shapes about 4 inches long onto greased baking trays. Chill.

Bake at 375°F for 10-12 minutes until pale golden. Transfer to a wire rack to cool.

Mix the confectioners' sugar with enough water to make a runny glaze and either dip the cookies in this or brush it over the tops. Finish with a scattering of sugar decorations on each and allow to set.

TOP: *Cane Cookies*
BOTTOM: *Lebkuchen*

CINNAMON STARS

Children will love to help make these cookies, which can be cut into different shapes and hung on the Christmas tree.

❖ ❖ ❖

2 CUPS SELF-RISING FLOUR

1 TABLESPOON GROUND CINNAMON

3/4 CUP BUTTER

1/2 CUP SUPERFINE SUGAR

1 TEASPOON GRATED ORANGE RIND

1 SMALL EGG, BEATEN

TO DECORATE

1 1/3 CUPS CONFECTIONERS' SUGAR

5-6 TEASPOONS ORANGE JUICE

SUGAR STRANDS OR SILVER BALLS

MAKES ABOUT 36-40

❖ ❖ ❖

Sift the flour and cinnamon into a bowl, rub in the butter until the mixture resembles fine crumbs. Stir in the sugar and orange rind, then bind together with the egg.

Knead the dough on a lightly floured surface, then cut out shapes such as stars, moons and Christmas trees, placing them on greased baking sheets. If wished, make a hole in each cookie with a skewer to thread with ribbon after baking and hang on the tree.

Bake the cookies at 350°F for 12-15 minutes. Transfer to a wire rack to cool.

Blend the orange juice into the confectioners' sugar to make a thick glaze, then use to spread over the cookies. Decorate with sugar strands or silver balls.

FESTIVE SPICY TWISTS

Make plenty of these cookies and put some in a pretty box to give away.

❖ ❖ ❖

2 1/2 CUPS SELF-RISING FLOUR

1 1/2 TEASPOONS APPLE PIE SPICE

1/2 TEASPOON GROUND GINGER

2/3 CUP BUTTER

2/3 CUP SIFTED RAW SUGAR

1 EGG, BEATEN

CONFECTIONERS' SUGAR TO DUST

MAKES 20

❖ ❖ ❖

Sift the flour and spices into a bowl. Add the butter and rub in until the mixture resembles fine crumbs. Stir in the sugar, then bind to a dough with the egg.

Divide the mixture into 20 pieces. Take each piece and roll into a rope about 8 inches long, then fold in half and twist.

Place the twists on greased baking sheets and refrigerate for 30 minutes.

Bake the cookies at 350°F for 12-15 minutes or until golden. Transfer to a wire rack to cool, then dust with confectioners' sugar.

TOP: *Cinnamon Stars*
BOTTOM: *Festive Spicy Twists*

NO-BAKE COOKIES

These are not cookies in the true sense, but they are so irresistible and so easy to make that it is well worth having a selection of recipes to choose from. Children will love making these as they use many of the most popular ingredients, including chocolate. Cooking is great fun for children, but basic safety in the kitchen is very important. Remind children to wash their hands before starting to prepare food and make sure you supervise young children while they are melting chocolate or using sharp knives to chop food or cut up cookies.

Follow the recipes carefully and always measure the ingredients; don't guess. When measuring syrup, rinse a table-spoon in very hot water before use, so that the syrup slides easily off the spoon. In some recipes, the chocolate is melt-ed in a saucepan with other ingredients. Otherwise, to melt chocolate, place in a bowl over a pan of simmering water, taking care not to let the water boil or splash into the bowl, or the chocolate will become thick and grainy.

Once prepared, these cookies are refrigerated until firm and are best stored in the refrigerator until needed to prevent them softening. Most of the recipes are ideal to make for children's parties, with one or two more sophisticated ones, such as Belgian Chocolate Slices, which could be served after dinner with coffee.

CONTENTS

CHOCOLATE TREATS

◆ ◆ ◆

8 SQUARES GERMAN SWEET CHOCOLATE

$^{1}/_{2}$ CUP BUTTER

2 TABLESPOONS LIGHT CORN SYRUP

$1^{1}/_{2}$ CUPS ROUGHLY BROKEN GRAHAM CRACKERS

$^{1}/_{3}$ CUP RAISINS OR GOLDEN RAISINS

$^{1}/_{2}$ CUP LIGHTLY TOASTED SLIVERED ALMONDS

3 TABLESPOONS FINELY CHOPPED
CANDIED CHERRIES

MAKES 12

◆ ◆ ◆

Put the chocolate, butter and syrup into a pan and heat very gently until melted. Stir in the crackers, raisins and almonds. Turn into a greased 7-inch shallow square pan and level the surface. Scatter over the chopped cherries and refrigerate to set. Cut into bars or squares.

GOLDEN CRACKLES

◆ ◆ ◆

$^{1}/_{4}$ CUP BUTTER

2 TABLESPOONS LIGHT CORN SYRUP

4 SQUARES GERMAN SWEET CHOCOLATE

$1^{3}/_{4}$ CUPS CORNFLAKES

$^{1}/_{4}$ CUP CHOPPED PEANUT KERNELS

MAKES 12

◆ ◆ ◆

Put the butter, syrup and chocolate into a pan. Heat gently until melted, then remove from the heat and stir in the cornflakes and nuts. Divide the mixture among 12 cupcake papers and refrigerate until set.

COCONUT DREAMS

◆ ◆ ◆

$^{1}/_{2}$ CUP BUTTER

2 CUPS CRUSHED SHORTCAKE COOKIES

3 TABLESPOONS UNSWEETENED COCOA

$^{2}/_{3}$ CUP SUPERFINE SUGAR

5 TABLESPOONS LIGHT CREAM

$1^{3}/_{4}$ CUPS SHREDDED COCONUT

3 TABLESPOONS CRUSHED PINEAPPLE, WELL DRAINED

6 SQUARES DARK CHOCOLATE

3 TABLESPOONS BUTTER

MAKES 18

◆ ◆ ◆

Melt the butter, then mix in the crushed cookies and cocoa. Press into the base of a 9-inch shallow square pan, lined with non-stick baking parchment paper. Refrigerate until firm.

Put the sugar and cream into a saucepan, stir over a low heat for 3-4 minutes. Cool slightly, then stir in the coconut and pineapple and spread over the base.

For the topping, put the chocolate and butter into a bowl over a pan of simmering water and stir until melted. Spread over the filling, then set in the refrigerator.

Use a hot knife to cut into squares.

TOP: *Chocolate Treats*
BOTTOM LEFT: *Coconut Dreams*
BOTTOM RIGHT: *Golden Crackles*

BUBBLE BARS

◆ ◆ ◆

1/3 CUP BUTTER

6 OUNCES MARSHMALLOWS

3 SQUARES GERMAN SWEET CHOCOLATE

3 1/2 CUPS RICE CRISPIES

MAKES 18

◆ ◆ ◆

Put the butter, marshmallows and chocolate into a pan, place over a low heat and allow to melt. Remove from the heat and stir in the rice crispies. Turn into a greased 7 x 11-inch shallow baking pan and press evenly. Leave to set, then cut into bars.

APRICOT CLUSTERS

◆ ◆ ◆

1/2 CUP BUTTER

2 TABLESPOONS LIGHT CORN SYRUP

4 SQUARES GERMAN SWEET CHOCOLATE

3/4 CUP CHOPPED READY-TO-EAT DRIED APRICOTS

2 CUPS LIGHTLY CRUSHED CRUNCHY OAT CEREAL

MAKES 12

◆ ◆ ◆

Melt the butter with the golden syrup and chocolate, allow to cool. Stir in the apricots and cereal, then divide among 12 cupcake papers. Refrigerate to set.

BUTTERSCOTCH FINGERS

◆ ◆ ◆

1/3 CUP BUTTER

1/2 CUP SIFTED RAW SUGAR

1 TABLESPOON LIGHT CORN SYRUP

1/2 CUP RAISINS

1/2 CUP CHOPPED HAZELNUTS

1 CUP LIGHTLY CRUSHED GRAHAM CRACKERS

1/3 CUP CHOPPED CANDIED CHERRIES

2 1/2 TABLESPOONS MIXED PEEL

MAKES 14

◆ ◆ ◆

Put the butter, sugar and syrup into a pan. Heat gently until the sugar dissolves, stirring all the time. Increase the heat and simmer for 2 minutes.

Stir in the remaining ingredients and mix well. Turn into a greased 7-inch shallow square pan and refrigerate to set. Cut into fingers to serve.

TOP: *Apricot Clusters*
BOTTOM LEFT: *Bubble Bars*
BOTTOM RIGHT: *Butterscotch Fingers*

CHERRY NUT BITES

◆ ◆ ◆

6 SQUARES WHITE CHOCOLATE

$1/_2$ CUP CHOPPED AND LIGHTLY TOASTED
MIXED NUTS

$1 1/_4$ CUPS SHREDDED COCONUT

$3/_4$ CUP CHOPPED CANDIED CHERRIES

MAKES 16

◆ ◆ ◆

Place the chocolate in a bowl over a pan of simmering water and stir until melted. Stir in the remaining ingredients, then turn into a 7-inch shallow square pan, lined with non-stick baking parchment paper. Refrigerate until set, then cut into squares.

BELGIAN CHOCOLATE SLICES

◆ ◆ ◆

8 SQUARES DARK CHOCOLATE

$1/_3$ CUP UNSALTED BUTTER

1 TABLESPOON LIGHT CORN SYRUP

2 TABLESPOONS LIGHT CREAM

$2/_3$ CUP CANDIED PINEAPPLE

$3/_4$ CUP CHOPPED WALNUTS OR PECANS

1 CUP LIGHTLY CRUSHED COCONUT COOKIES

2 TABLESPOONS SHREDDED COCONUT

MAKES 16 SLICES

◆ ◆ ◆

Put the chocolate, butter and syrup into a pan and heat gently until melted. Remove from the heat and stir in the cream, candied pineapple, nuts and cookies. Press evenly into an 8-inch greased loose-bottomed pie pan. Refrigerate to set. Remove the pan, decorate the edge with the coconut, then cut into slices.

NUTTY FUDGE TRIANGLES

◆ ◆ ◆

$1/_4$ CUP BUTTER

4 SQUARES GERMAN SWEET CHOCOLATE

2 CUPS CRUSHED GRAHAM CRACKERS

TOPPING

$1/_3$ CUP BUTTER

1 x 14 OUNCE CAN CONDENSED MILK

4 OUNCES FUDGE

$1/_2$ CUP CHOPPED AND LIGHTLY TOASTED NUTS

MAKES 30

◆ ◆ ◆

Put the butter and chocolate into a pan, stir over a low heat until melted. Mix in the crushed cookies then press evenly into a greased 7 x 11-inch shallow pan. Refrigerate until set.

For the topping, put the butter and condensed milk into a saucepan, bring to simmer, stirring, and cook for 4-5 minutes until very thick. Break up the fudge, add to the pan and stir until melted. Pour over the base, then scatter over the nuts. Refrigerate until set. Cut into 15 squares, then cut each in half to make triangles.

TOP: *Cherry Nut Bites*
CENTRE: *Nutty Fudge Triangles*
BOTTOM: *Belgian Chocolate Slices*

INDEX

ACKNOWLEDGMENTS

The author and publishers
would like to thank the following for their help
in the preparation of this book:

BERNDES
for supplying small cookie cutters

BILLINGTONS
for supplying unrefined sugars

LAKELAND PLASTICS
for supplying Airbake Cookie sheets